HOW SOFTWARE WORKS

The Magic Behind Encryption, CGI, Search Engines, and Other Everyday Technologies

by V. Anton Spraul

no starch press

San Francisco

HOW SOFTWARE WORKS. Copyright © 2015 by V. Anton Spraul.

Printed in USA

First printing

19 18 17 16 15   1 2 3 4 5 6 7 8 9

ISBN-10: 1-59327-666-4
ISBN-13: 978-1-59327-666-9

Text stock is SFI certified

Publisher: William Pollock
Production Editor: Alison Law
Cover Illustration: Josh Ellingson
Interior Design: Octopod Studios
Developmental Editors: Hayley Baker, Seph Kramer, and Greg Poulos
Technical Reviewer: Randall Hyde
Copyeditor: Rachel Monaghan
Compositor: Susan Glinert Stevens
Proofreader: James Fraleigh

For information on distribution, translations, or bulk sales, please contact No Starch Press, Inc. directly:

No Starch Press, Inc.
245 8th Street, San Francisco, CA 94103
phone: 415.863.9900; info@nostarch.com
www.nostarch.com

Library of Congress Cataloging-in-Publication Data:

Spraul, V. Anton.
  How software works : the magic behind encryption, CGI, search engines, and other everyday technologies / by
V. Anton Spraul.
       pages cm
  Includes index.
  Summary: "A guide for non-technical readers that explores topics like data encryption; computer graphics
creation; password protection; video compression; how data is found in huge databases; how programs can work
together on the same problem without conflict; and how map software finds routes."-- Provided by publisher.
   ISBN 978-1-59327-666-9 -- ISBN 1-59327-666-4
  1. Electronic data processing--Popular works. 2. Computer software--Popular works. 3. Computer networks--
Popular works. I. Title.
  QA76.5.S6663 2015
  005.3--dc23
                                    2015022623

About the Author

V. Anton Spraul has taught introductory programming and computer science to students from all over the world for more than 15 years. He is also the author of *Think Like a Programmer* (No Starch Press) and *Computer Science Made Simple* (Broadway).

About the Technical Reviewer

Randall Hyde is the author of *The Art of Assembly Language* and *Write Great Code* (both No Starch Press), and is also the co-author of *The Waite Group's Microsoft Macro Assembler 6.0 Bible* (Sams Publishing). Hyde taught assembly language at the University of California, Riverside, for more than a decade and has been programming software for nuclear reactor consoles for the past 12 years.

BRIEF CONTENTS

CONTENTS IN DETAIL

5
GAME GRAPHICS
85

6
DATA COMPRESSION
115

ACKNOWLEDGMENTS

This book was shaped and guided by a platoon of talented editors: Alison Law, Greg Poulos, Seph Kramer, Hayley Baker, Randall Hyde, Rachel Monaghan, and the "Big Fish" of No Starch, Bill Pollock. Beyond the editorial staff, I appreciate the support and kindness of everyone I've worked with at No Starch.

    The two people who helped me the most, though, are Mary Beth and Madeline, the best wife and daughter I can imagine. Without their love and support, this book would not have been written.

INTRODUCTION

Science fiction author Arthur C. Clarke wrote that "any sufficiently advanced technology is indistinguishable from magic." If we don't know how something works, then it might as well be explained by supernatural forces. By that standard, we live in an age of magic.

Software is woven into our lives, into everyday things like online transactions, special effects in movies, and streaming video. We're forgetting we used to live in a world in which the answer to a question wasn't just a Google search away, or where finding a route for a car trip began with unfolding a cumbersome map.

But few of us have any idea how all this software works. Unlike many innovations of the past, you can't take software apart to see what it's doing. Everything happens on a computer chip that looks the same whether the device is performing an amazing task or isn't even turned on. Knowing how a program works seems to require spending years of study to become a programmer. So it's no wonder that many of us assume that software is beyond our understanding, a collection of secrets known only to a technological elite. But that's wrong.

Who This Book Is For

Anyone can learn how software works. All you need is curiosity. Whether you're a casual fan of technology, a programmer in the making, or someone in between, this book is for you.

This book covers the most commonly used processes in software and does so without a single line of programming code. No prior knowledge of how computers operate is required. To make this possible, I've simplified a few processes and clipped some details, but that doesn't mean these are mere high-level overviews; you'll be getting the real goods, with enough details that you'll truly understand how these programs do what they do.

Topics Covered

Computers are so ubiquitous in the modern world that the list of subjects I could cover seems endless. I've chosen topics that are most central to our daily lives and with the most interesting explanations.

- **Chapter 1:** *Encryption* allows us to scramble our data so that only we can access it. When you lock your phone or password-protect a *.zip* file, you're using encryption. We'll see how different scrambling techniques are combined in modern encryption software.

- **Chapter 2:** *Passwords* are the keys we use to lock our data and how we identify ourselves to remote systems. You'll see how passwords are used in encryption and learn the surprising steps that must be taken to keep passwords safe from attackers.

- **Chapter 3:** *Web Security* is what we need to safely purchase goods online or access our accounts. Locking data for transmission requires a different method of scrambling called public-key encryption. You'll discover how a secure web session requires all the techniques covered in the first three chapters.

- **Chapter 4:** *Movie CGI* is pure software magic, creating whole worlds out of mathematical descriptions. You'll discover how software took over traditional cel animation and then learn the key concepts behind making a complete movie set with software.

- **Chapter 5:** *Video Game Graphics* are impressive not just for their visuals but also for how they are created in mere fractions of a second. We'll explore a host of clever tricks games use to produce stunning images when they don't have time for the techniques discussed in the previous chapter.

- **Chapter 6: *Data Compression*** shrinks data so that we can get more out of our storage and bandwidth limits. We'll explore the best methods for shrinking data, and then see how they are combined to compress high-definition video for Blu-ray discs and web streams.

- **Chapter 7: *Search*** is about finding data instantly, whether it's a search for a file on our own computer or a search across the whole Web. We'll explore how data is organized for quick searches, how search zeros in on requested data, and how web searches return the most useful results.

- **Chapter 8: *Concurrency*** allows multiple programs to share data. Without concurrency, multiplayer video games wouldn't be possible, and online bank systems could allow only one customer at a time. We'll talk about the methods that enable different processors to access the same data without getting in each other's way.

- **Chapter 9: *Map Routes*** are those instant directions we get from mapping sites and in-car navigators. You'll discover what a map looks like to software and the specialized search techniques that find the best routes.

Behind the Magic

I think it's important to share this knowledge. We shouldn't have to live in a world we don't understand, and it's becoming impossible to understand the modern world without also understanding software. Clarke's message can be taken as a warning that those who understand technology can fool those who don't. For example, a company may claim that the theft of its login data poses little danger to its customers. Could this be true, and how? After reading this book, you'll know the answer to questions like these.

Beyond that, though, there's an even better reason to learn the secrets of how software works: because those secrets are *really cool*. I think the best magic tricks are even more magical once you learn how they are done. Read on and you'll see what I mean.

1

ENCRYPTION

We rely on software to protect our data every day, but most of us know little about how this protection works. Why does a "lock" icon in the corner of your browser mean it's safe to enter your credit card number? How does creating a password for your phone actually protect the data inside? What really prevents other people from logging into your online accounts?

Computer security is the science of protecting data. In a way, computer security represents technology solving a problem that technology created. Not that long ago, most data wasn't stored digitally. We had filing cabinets in our offices and shoeboxes of photographs under our beds. Of course, back then you couldn't easily share your photographs with friends around the world or check your bank balance from a mobile phone, but neither could anyone steal your private data without physically taking it. Today, not only can you be robbed at a distance, but you might not even know you've been robbed—that is, until your bank calls to ask why you are buying thousands of dollars in gift cards.

Over these first three chapters, we'll discuss the most important concepts behind computer security. In this chapter, we talk about encryption. By itself, encryption provides us with the capability to lock our data so only *we* can unlock it. Additional techniques, discussed in the next two chapters, are needed to provide the full security suite that we depend on, but encryption is the core of computer security.

The Goal of Encryption

Think of a file on your computer: it might contain text, a photograph, a spreadsheet, audio, or video. You want to access the file but keep it secret from everyone else. This is the fundamental problem of computer security. To keep the file secret, you can use *encryption* to transform it into a new format that is unreadable until the file has been returned to its original form using *decryption*. The original file is the *plaintext* (even if the file isn't text), and the encrypted file is the *ciphertext*.

An *attacker* is someone who attempts to decrypt the ciphertext without authorization. The goal of encryption is to create a ciphertext that is easy for authorized users to decrypt, while practically impossible for attackers to decrypt. "Practically" is the source of many headaches for security researchers. Just as no lock is absolutely unbreakable, no encryption can be absolutely impossible to decrypt. With enough time and enough computing power, any encryption scheme can be broken in theory. The goal of computer security is to make an attacker's job so difficult that successful attacks are impossible in practice, requiring computing resources beyond an attacker's means.

Rather than jump headfirst into the intricacies of software-based encryption, I'll start this chapter with some simple examples from the presoftware days of codes and spies. Although the strength of encryption has vastly improved over the years, these same classic techniques form the basis of all encryption. Later, you'll see how these ideas are combined in a modern digital encryption scheme.

Transposition: Same Data, Different Order

One of the simplest ways to encrypt data is called *transposition*, which simply means "changing position." Transposition is the kind of encryption my friends and I used when passing notes in grade school. Because these notes were passed through untrustworthy hands, it was imperative the notes were unintelligible to anyone but us.

To keep messages secret, we rearranged the order of the letters using a simple, easy-to-reverse scheme. Suppose I needed to share the vital intelligence that CATHY LIKES KEITH (the names have been changed to protect the innocent). To encrypt the message, I copied every third letter of the plaintext (ignoring any spaces). During the first pass through the message, I copied five letters, as shown in Figure 1-1.

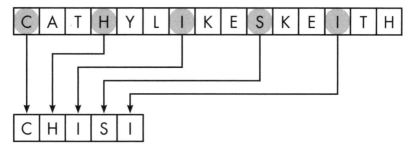

Figure 1-1: The first pass in the transposition of the sample message

Having reached the end of the message, I started back at the beginning and continued selecting every third remaining letter. The second pass got me to the state shown in Figure 1-2.

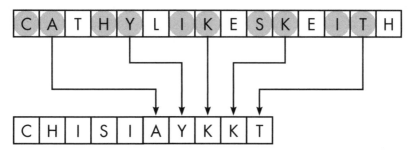

Figure 1-2: The second transposition pass

On the last pass I copied the remaining letters, as shown in Figure 1-3.

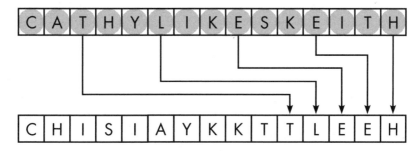

Figure 1-3: The final transposition pass

The resulting ciphertext is CHISIAYKKTTLEEH. My friends could read the message by reversing the transposition process. The first step is shown in Figure 1-4. Returning all the letters to their original position reveals the plaintext.

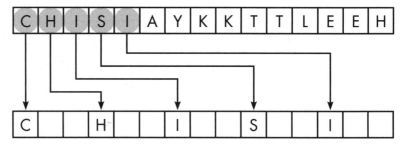

Figure 1-4: The first pass in reversing the transposition for decryption

This basic transposition method was fun to use, but it's terribly weak encryption. The biggest concern is a leak—one of my friends blabbing about the encryption method to someone outside the circle. Once that happens, sending encrypted messages won't be secure anymore; it will just be more work. Leaks are sadly inevitable—and not just with schoolchildren. Every encryption method is vulnerable to leaks, and the more people use a particular method, the more likely it will leak.

For this reason, all good encryption systems follow a rule formulated by early Dutch cryptographer Auguste Kerckhoffs, known as *Kerckhoffs's principle*: the security of data should not depend on the encryption method remaining a secret.

Cipher Keys

This raises an obvious question. If the encryption method is not a secret, how do we securely encrypt data? The answer lies in following a general, publically disclosed encryption method, but varying the encryption of individual messages using a *cipher key* (or just *key*). To understand what a key is, let's examine a more general transposition method.

In this method, senders and receivers share a secret number prior to sending any messages. Let's say my friends and I agree on 374. We'll use this number to alter the transposition pattern in our ciphertexts. This pattern is shown in Figure 1-5 for the message CATHY LIKES KEITH. The digits of our secret number dictate which letter should be copied from the plaintext to the ciphertext. Because the first digit is 3, the third letter of the plaintext, *T*, becomes the first letter of the ciphertext. The next digit is 7, so the next letter is the seventh letter after the *T*, which is *S*. Next, we select the fourth letter from the *S*. The first three letters of the ciphertext are *TST*.

Figure 1-6 shows how the next two letters are copied to the ciphertext. Starting from where we left off (indicated by the circled 1 in the figure), we count three positions, returning to the beginning of the plaintext when we reach the end, to select *A* as the fourth letter of the ciphertext. The next letter chosen is seven positions after the *A*, skipping letters that have already been copied: the *K*. The process continues until all of the letters of the plaintext have been transposed.

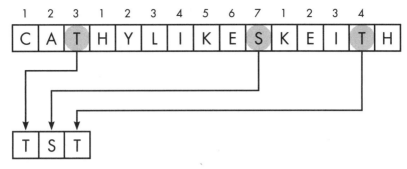

Figure 1-5: The first pass in transposing using the key 374

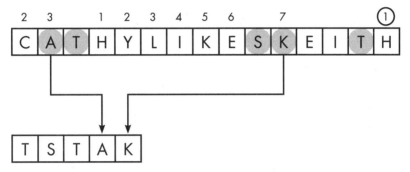

Figure 1-6: The second pass in transposing using the key 374

The secret number 374, then, is our cipher key. Someone who intercepts this message won't be able to decrypt it without the key, even if they understand we're using a transposition method. The code can be regularly changed to prevent blabbermouths and turncoats from compromising the encryption.

Attacking the Encryption

Even without the key, attackers can still try to recover the plaintext through other means. Encrypted data can be attacked through *brute force*, trying all the possible ways of applying the encryption method to the ciphertext. For a message encrypted using transposition, a brute-force attack would examine all permutations of the ciphertext. Because brute force is almost always an option, the number of trials an attacker will need to find the plaintext is a good baseline for encryption strength. In our example, the message CATHY LIKES KEITH has around 40 billion permutations.

That's a huge number, so instead of brute force, a smart attacker would apply some common sense to recover the plaintext faster. If the attacker can assume the plaintext is in English, then most of the permutations can be ruled out before they are tested. For example, the attacker can assume the plaintext won't start with the letters *HT* because no English word starts with those letters. That's a billion permutations the attacker won't have to check.

An attacker with some idea of the words in the message can be even smarter about figuring out the plaintext. In our example, the attacker might guess the message includes the name of a classmate. They can see what names can be formed from the ciphertext letters and then determine what words can be formed from the leftover letters.

Guesses about the plaintext content are known as *cribs*. The strongest kind of crib is a *known-plaintext attack*. To carry out this type of attack, the attacker must have access to a plaintext A, its matching ciphertext A, and a ciphertext B that uses the same cipher key as ciphertext A. Although this scenario sounds unlikely, it does happen. People often leave documents unguarded when they are no longer considered secret without realizing they may aid attacks on other documents. Known-plaintext attacks are powerful; figuring out the transposition pattern is easy when you have both the plaintext and ciphertext in front of you.

The best defenses against known-plaintext attacks are good security practices, such as regularly changing passwords. Even with the best security practices, though, attackers will almost always have some idea of a plaintext's contents (that's why are they so interested in reading it). In many cases, they will know most of the plaintext and may have access to known plaintext-ciphertext pairs. A good encryption system should render cribs and known plaintexts useless to attackers.

Substitution: Replacing Data

The other fundamental encryption technique is more resistant to cribs. Instead of moving the data around, *substitution* methods systematically replace individual pieces of data. With text messages, the simplest form of substitution replaces every occurrence of one letter with another letter. For example, every A becomes a D, every B an H, and so on. A key for this type of encryption looks like Table 1-1.

Table 1-1: A Substitution Cipher Key

Original	A	B	C	D	E	F	G	H	I	J	K	L	M	N	O	P	Q	R	S	T	U	V	W	X	Y	Z
Replacement	M	N	B	V	C	X	Z	L	K	F	H	G	J	D	S	A	P	O	I	U	Y	T	R	E	W	Q

Although *simple substitution*, as this method is called, is an improvement over transposition, it too has problems: there are only so many possible substitutions, so an attacker can sometimes decrypt ciphertext through brute force.

Simple substitution is also vulnerable to *frequency analysis*, in which an attacker applies knowledge of how often letters or letter combinations occur in a given language. Stated broadly, knowing how often data items are likely to appear in a plaintext gives the attacker an advantage. For example, the letter *E* is the most common letter in English writing, and *TH* is the most common letter pair. Therefore, the most frequently occurring letter in a long ciphertext is likely to represent plaintext *E*, and the most frequently occurring letter pair is likely to represent plaintext *TH*.

The power of frequency analysis means that substitution encryption becomes more vulnerable as the text grows longer. Attacks are also easier when a collection of ciphertexts is known to have been encrypted with the same key; avoiding such *key reuse* is an important security practice.

Varying the Substitution Pattern

To strengthen encryption against frequency analysis, we can vary the substitution pattern during encryption, so the first *E* in the plaintext might be replaced with *A*, but the second *E* in the plaintext is replaced with a *T*. This technique is known as *polyalphabetic substitution*. One method of polyalphabetic substitution uses a grid of alphabets known as a *tabula recta*, shown in Figure 1-7. In this table, each row and column is labeled with the letter of the alphabet that starts the row or column. Every location in the grid is located with two letters, such as row D, column H, which contains the letter *K*.

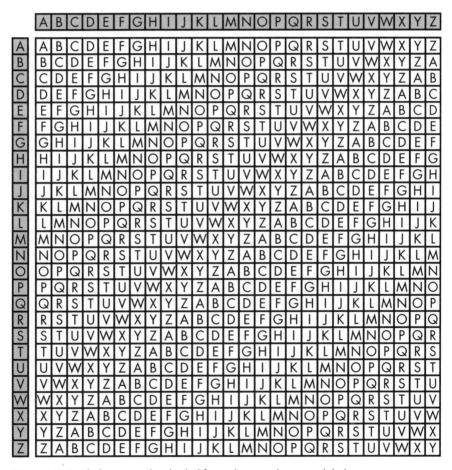

Figure 1-7: A tabula recta—the shaded first column and row are labels.

When using a tabula recta, the key is textual—letters are used to vary the encryption instead of numbers, as we used in our transposition example.

The letters of the plaintext select rows in the tabula recta, and the letters of the key select columns. For example, suppose our plaintext message is the word *SECRET*, and our encryption key is the word *TOUGH*. Because the first letter of the plaintext is *S* and the first letter of the key is *T*, the first letter of the ciphertext is found at row S, column T in the tabula recta: the letter *L*. We then use the O column of the table to encrypt the second plaintext letter *E* (resulting in *S*), and so on, as shown in Figure 1-8. Because the plaintext is longer than the key, we must reuse the first letter of the key.

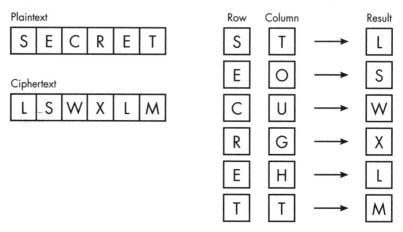

Figure 1-8: Encryption using the tabula recta and cipher key TOUGH

Decryption reverses the process, as shown in Figure 1-9. The letters in the key indicate the columns, which are scanned to find the corresponding letter in the ciphertext. The row where the ciphertext letter is found indicates the plaintext letter. In our example, the first letter of our key is *T*, and the first letter of the ciphertext is *L*. We scan the T column of the tabula recta to find *L*; because *L* appears in row S, the plaintext letter is *S*. The process repeats for every letter of the ciphertext.

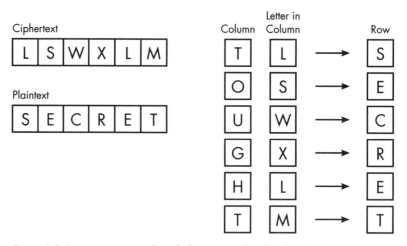

Figure 1-9: Decryption using the tabula recta and cipher key TOUGH

Polyalphabetic substitution is more effective than simple substitution because it varies the substitution pattern throughout the message. In our example, the two occurrences of *E* in the plaintext become different ciphertext letters, and the two occurrences of *L* in the ciphertext represent two different plaintext letters.

Key Expansion

Although polyalphabetic substitution is a great improvement over simple substitution, it's effective only when the key isn't repeated too often; otherwise it has the same problems as simple substitution. With a key length of five, for example, each plaintext letter would be represented by only five different ciphertext letters, leaving long ciphertexts vulnerable to frequency analysis and cribs. An attacker would have to work harder, but given enough ciphertext to work with, an attacker could still break the encryption.

For maximum effectiveness, we need encryption keys that are as long as the plaintext, a technique known as a *one-time pad*. But that's not a practical solution for most situations. Instead, a method called *key expansion* allows short keys to do the work of longer ones. One implementation of this idea frequently appears in spy novels. Instead of sharing a super-long key, two spies who need to exchange messages agree on a *code book*, which is used as a repository of long keys. To avoid arousing suspicion, the code book is an ordinary piece of literature, like a specific edition of Shakespeare's plays.

Let's suppose a 50-letter message will be sent using this scheme. In addition to the ciphertext, the message sender also appends the unexpanded key. Using the works of Shakespeare as the code book, the unexpanded key might be 2.2.4.9. The first 2 indicates the second of Shakespeare's plays when listed alphabetically (*As You Like It*). The second 2 means Act II of the play. The 4 means Scene 4 of that act. The 9 means the ninth sentence of that scene in the specified edition: "When I was at home, I was in a better place, but travelers must be content." The number of letters in this sentence exceeds the number in the plaintext and could be used for encryption and decryption using a tabula recta as before. In this way, a relatively short key can be expanded to fit a particular message.

Note that this scheme doesn't qualify as a one-time pad because the code book is finite, and therefore the sentence-keys would have to be reused eventually. But it does mean our spies only have to remember short cipher keys while encrypting their messages more securely with longer keys. As you'll see, the key expansion concept is important in computer encryption because the cipher keys required are huge but need to be stored in smaller forms.

The Advanced Encryption Standard

Now that we've seen how transposition, substitution, and key expansion work individually, let's see how secure digital encryption results from a careful combination of all three techniques.

The *Advanced Encryption Standard (AES)* is an open standard, which means the specifications may be implemented by anyone without paying a license fee. Whether you realize it or not, much of your data is protected by AES. If you have a secure wireless network at your home or office, if you have ever password-protected a file in a *.zip* archive, or if you use a credit card at a store or make a withdrawal from an ATM, you are probably relying, at least in part, on AES.

Binary Basics

Up to now, I've used text encryption samples to keep the examples simple. The data encrypted by computers, though, is represented in the form of binary numbers. If you haven't worked with these numbers before, here's an introduction.

Decimal Versus Binary

The number system we all grew up with is called the *decimal* system, *deci* meaning "ten," because the system uses 10 digits, 0 through 9. Each digit in a number represents the quantity of a unit 10 times greater than the digit to its right. The units and quantities for the decimal number 23,065 are shown in Figure 1-10. The 2 in the fifth position from the left means we have 2 "ten thousands," for example, and the 6 means 6 "tens."

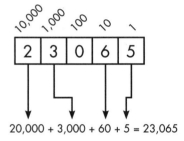

$$20,000 + 3,000 + 60 + 5 = 23,065$$

Figure 1-10: Each digit in the decimal number 23,065 represents a different unit quantity.

In the *binary* number system, there are only two possible digits, 0 or 1, which are called *bits*, for *bi*nary dig*its*. Each bit in a binary number represents a unit twice as large as the bit to the right. The units and quantities for the binary number 110101 are shown in Figure 1-11. As shown, we have one of each of the following units: 32, 16, 4, and 1. Therefore, the binary number 110101 represents the sum of these four unit values, which is the decimal number 53.

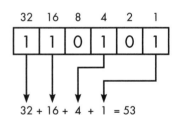

$$32 + 16 + 4 + 1 = 53$$

Figure 1-11: Each bit in the binary number 110101 represents a different unit quantity.

Binary numbers are often written with a fixed number of bits. The most common length for a binary number is eight bits, known as a *byte*. Although the decimal number 53 can be written as 110101 in binary, writing 53 as a byte requires eight bits, so leading 0 bits fill out the other positions to make 00110101. The smallest byte value, 00000000, represents decimal 0; the largest possible byte, 11111111, represents decimal 255.

Bitwise Operations

Along with the usual mathematical operations such as addition and multiplication, software also uses some operations unique to binary numbers. These are known as *bitwise operations* because they are applied individually to each bit rather than to the binary number as whole.

The bitwise operation known as *exclusive-or*, or *XOR*, is common in encryption. When two binary numbers are XORed together, the 1s in the second number flip the corresponding bits in the first number, as shown in Figure 1-12.

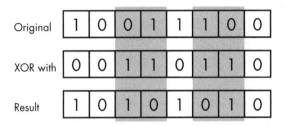

Figure 1-12: The exclusive-or (XOR) operation. The 1 bits in the second byte indicate which bits are "flipped" in the first byte, as shown in the shaded columns.

Remember, encryption must be reversible. XOR alters the bit patterns in a way that's impossible to predict without knowing the binary numbers involved, but it's easily reversed. XORing the result with the second number flips the same bits back to their original state, as shown in Figure 1-13.

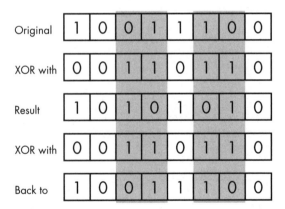

Figure 1-13: If we XOR a byte with the same byte twice, we're back to where we started.

Converting Data to Binary Form

Computers use binary numbers to represent all kinds of data. A plaintext file could be a text message, a spreadsheet, an image, an audio file, or anything else—but in the end, every file is a sequence of bytes. Most computer data is already numeric and can therefore be directly converted into binary numbers. In some cases, though, a special encoding system is needed to convert non-numeric data into binary form.

For example, to see how a text message becomes a sequence of bytes, consider this message:

Send more money!

This message has 16 characters, counting the letters, spaces, and exclamation point. We can turn each character into a byte using a system such as the *American Standard Code for Information Interchange*, which is always referred to by its acronym, *ASCII*, pronounced "as-key". In ASCII, capital *A* is represented by the number 65, *B* by 66, and so on, through 90 for *Z*. Table 1-2 shows some selected entries from the ASCII table.

Table 1-2: Selected Entries from the ASCII Table

Character	Decimal number	Binary byte
(space)	32	00100000
!	33	00100001
,	44	00101100
.	46	00101110
A	65	01000001
B	66	01000010
C	67	01000011
D	68	01000100
E	69	01000101
a	97	01100001
b	98	01100010
c	99	01100011
d	100	01100100
e	101	01100101

AES Encryption: The Big Picture

Before we examine the details of AES encryption, here's an overview of the process.

Cipher keys in AES are binary numbers. The size of the key can vary, but we'll discuss the simplest version of AES, which uses a 128-bit key. Using mathematical key expansion, AES transforms the original 128-bit key into eleven 128-bit keys.

AES divides plaintext data into blocks of 16 bytes in a 4×4 grid; the grid for the sample message *Send more money!* is shown in Figure 1-14. Heavy lines separate the 16 bytes, and light lines separate the bits within the bytes.

```
0 1 0 1 0 0 0 1 1 0 1 1 0 0 1 0 1 0 1 1 1 0 1 1 1 0 0 1 1 0 0 1 0 0
0 0 1 0 0 0 0 0 0 1 1 0 1 1 0 1 0 1 1 0 1 1 1 1 0 1 1 1 1 0 0 1 0
0 1 1 0 0 1 0 1 0 0 1 0 0 0 0 0 0 1 1 0 1 1 0 1 0 1 1 1 0 1 1 1 1 1
0 1 1 0 1 1 1 1 0 0 1 1 0 0 1 0 1 0 1 1 1 1 1 0 0 1 0 0 1 0 0 0 0 1
```

Figure 1-14: The sample message Send more money! *transformed into a grid of bytes, ready for encryption using AES*

The plaintext data is divided into as many 16-byte blocks as necessary. If the last block isn't full, the rest of the block is padded with random binary numbers.

AES then subjects each 16-byte block of plaintext data to 10 *rounds* of encryption. During a round, the bytes are transposed within the block and substituted using a table. Then, using the XOR operation, the bytes in the block are combined with each other and with one of the 128-bit keys.

That's AES in a nutshell; now let's look at some of these steps in more detail.

Key Expansion in AES

Key expansion in a digital encryption system is a bit different than the "code book" concept we discussed earlier. Instead of just looking up a longer key in a book, AES expands the key using the same tools it will later use for the encryption itself: the binary XOR operation, transposition, and simple substitution.

Figure 1-15 shows the first few stages of the key expansion process. Each of the blocks in the figure is 32 bits, and one row in this figure represents one 128-bit key. The original 128-bit key makes up the first four blocks, which are shaded in the figure. Every other block is the result of an XOR between two previous blocks; the XOR operation is represented by a plus sign in a circle. Block 6, for example, results from the XOR of Block 2 and Block 5.

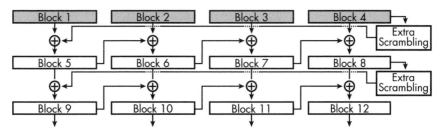

Figure 1-15: Key expansion process for AES

As you can see on the right of the figure, every fourth block passes through a box labeled "Extra Scrambling." This process includes transposing the bytes inside the block and substituting each byte according to a table called the *S-box*.

The S-box table, which is used both in the key expansion and later in the encryption itself, is carefully designed to amplify differences in the plaintext. That is, two plaintext bytes that are similar will tend to have S-box replacements that are quite different. The first eight entries from the table are shown in Table 1-3.

Table 1-3: Excerpts from the S-Box Table

Original bit pattern	Replacement bit pattern
00000000	01100011
00000001	01111100
00000010	01110111
00000011	01111011
00000100	11110010
00000101	01101011
00000110	01101111
00000111	11000101
00001000	00110000
00001001	00000001

AES Encryption Rounds

Once AES has all the required keys, the real encryption can begin. Recall that the binary plaintext is stored in a grid of 16 bytes or 128 bits, which is the same size as the original key. This is not a coincidence. The first step of the actual encryption is to XOR the 128-bit data grid with the original 128-bit key. Now the work begins in earnest, as the data grid is subjected to 10 rounds of number crunching. There are four steps in each round.

1. Substitution.
Each of the 16 bytes in the grid is replaced using the same S-box table used in the key expansion process.

2. Row Transposition.
Next, the bytes are moved to different positions within their row in the grid.

3. Column Combination.
Next, for each byte in the grid, a new byte is calculated from a combination of all four bytes in that column. This computation involves the XOR operation again, but also a binary form of transposition. To give you the flavor of the process, Figure 1-16 shows the computation of the leftmost byte in the lowest row. The four bytes of the leftmost column are XORed together, but the top and bottom bytes in the column have their bits transposed first. This kind of transposition is known as *bitwise rotation*; the bits slide one position to the left, with the leftmost bit moving over to the right end.

Every byte in the new grid is computed in a similar way, by combining the bytes in the column using XOR; the only variation is which bytes have their bits rotated before the XOR.

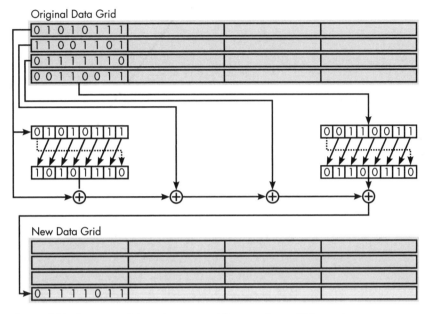

Figure 1-16: One part of the column-scrambling step in an AES round

4. XOR with Cipher Key.

Finally, the grid that results from the previous step is XORed with the key for that round. This is why key expansion is needed, so that each round XORs with a different key.

The AES decryption process performs the same steps as the encryption process, in reverse. Because the only operations in the encryption are XORs, simple substitution from the S-box, and transpositions of bits and bytes, everything is reversible if the key is known.

Block Chaining

AES encryption could be applied individually to each 16-byte block in a file, but this would create vulnerabilities in the ciphertext. As we've discussed, the more times an encryption key is used, the more likely it is that attackers will discover and exploit patterns. Computer files are often enormous, and using the same key to encrypt millions of blocks is a form of large-scale key reuse that exposes the ciphertext to frequency analysis and related techniques.

For this reason, block-based encryption systems like AES are modified so that identical blocks in plaintext produce different ciphertext blocks. One such modification is called *block chaining*.

When block chaining, the first block of the plaintext is XORed with a random 128-bit number before encryption. This random number is called the *starting variable* and is stored along with the ciphertext. Because each encryption is assigned a random starting variable, two files that begin with the same data will have different ciphertexts even when encrypted with the same key.

Every subsequent plaintext block is XORed with the previous ciphertext block before encryption, "chaining" the encryption as shown in Figure 1-17. Chaining ensures that duplicate blocks in a plaintext will result in different ciphertext blocks. This means files of any length can be encrypted without fear of frequency analysis.

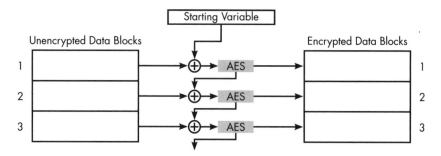

Figure 1-17: AES encryption using block chaining

Why AES Is Secure

As you can see, although AES contains many steps, each individual step is just transposition or simple substitution. Why is AES considered strong enough to protect the world's data? Remember, attackers use brute force or cribs, or exploit patterns in the ciphertext. AES has excellent defenses against all of these attack methods.

With AES, brute force means running the ciphertext through the decryption process with every possible key until the plaintext is produced. In AES, keys have 128, 192, or 256 bits. Even the smallest key size offers around 300,000,000,000,000,000,000,000,000,000,000,000,000 possible keys, and a brute-force attack would need to try about half of these before it could expect to hit the right one. An attacker with a computer that could try a million keys per second could, in a day, try 1,000,000 keys × 60 seconds × 60 minutes × 24 hours = 86,400,000,000 keys. In a year, the attacker could try 31,536,000,000,000 keys. Although that's a large number, it's not even a billionth of a billionth of the possible combinations. An attacker might acquire more computing power, but trying that many keys still doesn't seem feasible—and that's just for the 128-bit version.

AES also makes using cribs or finding exploitable patterns difficult. During each encryption round, AES rotates the bytes in each row of the grid and combines the bytes in each column. After many rounds of this, the bytes are thoroughly mixed together so the final value of any one byte in the ciphertext grid depends on the initial plaintext values of all the bytes in a grid. This encryption property is called *diffusion*.

Furthermore, passing the bytes through the S-box, round after round, amplifies the effect of diffusion, and block chaining passes the diffusion effects of each block on to the next. Together, these operations give AES the *avalanche* property, in which small changes in the plaintext result in sweeping changes throughout the ciphertext.

AES thwarts attackers no matter how much they know about the general layout of the plaintext. For example, a company may send emails to customers based on a common template, in which the only variables are the customers' account numbers and outstanding balances. With diffusion, avalanches, and block chaining, the ciphertexts of these emails will be very different. Diffusion and avalanches also reduce patterns that could be exploited through frequency analysis. Even a huge plaintext file consisting of the same 16-byte block repeated over and over would result in a random-looking jumble of bits when run through AES encryption with block chaining.

Possible AES Attacks

AES appears to be strong against conventional encryption attacks, but are there hidden weaknesses that offer shortcuts to finding the right cipher key? The answer is unclear because proving a negative is difficult. Stating that no shortcuts, or *cracks*, are known to exist is one thing; proving they *couldn't* exist is another. Cryptography is a science, and science is always expanding its boundaries. We simply don't understand cryptography and its underlying mathematics to a point where we can say what's impossible.

Part of the difficulty in analyzing the vulnerabilities of an open standard like AES is that programmers implementing the standard in code may unwittingly introduce security flaws. For example, some AES implementations are vulnerable to a *timing attack*, in which an attacker gleans information about the data being encrypted by measuring how long the encryption takes. The attacker must have access to the specific computer on which the encryption is performed, however, so this isn't really a flaw in the underlying encryption, but that's no comfort if security is compromised.

The best-understood vulnerability of AES is known as a *related-key attack*. When two keys are mathematically related in a specific way, an attacker can sometimes use knowledge gathered from messages encrypted using one key to recover a message encrypted using the other key. Researchers have discovered a way to recover the AES encryption key for a particular ciphertext in less time than a brute-force attack, but the method requires ciphertexts of the same plaintext encrypted with keys that are related to the original key in very specific ways.

Although this shortcut counts as a crack, it may not be of practical value to attackers. First of all, although it greatly reduces the amount of work to recover the original key, it may not be feasible for any existing computer or network of computers. Second, it's not easy to obtain the other ciphertexts that have been encrypted with the related keys; it requires a breakdown in the implementation or use of the cipher. Therefore, this crack is currently considered theoretical, not a practical weakness of the system.

Perhaps the most worrying aspect of this crack is that it's believed to work only for the supposedly stronger 256-bit-key version of AES, not the simpler 128-bit-key version described in this chapter. This demonstrates perhaps the greatest weakness of modern encryption techniques: their complexity. Flaws can go undetected for years despite the efforts of expert reviewers; small changes in the design can have large ramifications for security; and features intended to increase security may have the opposite effect.

The Limits of Private-Key Encryption

The real limitation of an encryption method like AES, though, has nothing to do with a potential hidden flaw.

All the encryption methods in this chapter, AES included, are known as *symmetric-key* methods—this means the key that encrypts a message or file is the same key that is used to decrypt it. If you want to use AES to encrypt a file on your desktop's hard drive or the contact list in your phone, that's not a problem; only you are locking and unlocking the data. But what happens when you need to secure a data transmission, as when you enter your credit card number on a retail website? You could encrypt the data with AES and send it to the website, but the software on the website couldn't decrypt the ciphertext without the key.

This is the *shared key problem*, and it's one of the central problems of cryptography. Without a secure way to share keys, symmetric key encryption, by itself, is only useful for locking one's own private data. Encrypting data for transmission requires a different approach, using different keys for encryption and decryption—you'll see how this is done in Chapter 3.

But there's another problem we need to tackle first. AES requires an enormous binary number as a key, but users can't be expected to memorize a string of 128 bits. Instead, we memorize passwords. As it turns out, the secure storage and use of passwords presents its own quandaries. Those are the subject of the next chapter.

2

PASSWORDS

One of software's most crucial tasks is the protection of passwords. That may be surprising. After all, aren't passwords part of systems that *provide* protection? Don't passwords secure our accounts with banks, web retailers, and online games?

The truth is, while passwords are the keystones of computer security, they can become the targets of attacks. If a remote computer accepts your identity based on your password, a process known as *authentication*, it must have a list of user passwords to compare against. That password list is a tempting target for attackers. Recent years have seen a number of large-scale thefts of customer account data. How does this happen, and what can be done to make breaches less likely? That's what this chapter is about.

Before you learn how passwords are protected, though, you'll see how they are transformed into binary numbers, a process that has important implications for both password storage and encryption.

Transforming a Password into a Number

In Chapter 1, you saw how an individual character could be replaced by a number from the ASCII table. Here, you'll see how a string of characters can be replaced by one big number, such as the 128-bit key we need for AES. In computing, transforming something into a number in a specified range is called *hashing*, and the resulting number is called a *hash code, hash value,* or just plain *hash.*

Here, the word *hash* means chopping something up and then cramming the pieces back together, as with hash browns. A particular hashing method is known as a *hash function.* Hashing a password always begins by converting each character in the password to a number using an encoding system such as ASCII. Hash functions differ in how they combine those numbers; the hash functions used in encryption and authentication systems must be carefully designed or security may be compromised.

Properties of Good Hash Functions

Developing a good hash function is no easy task. To understand what hash functions are up against, consider the short password *dog.* That word contains 3 ASCII bytes, or a mere 24 bits of data, while an AES key is a minimum of 128 bits. Therefore a good hash function must be capable of transforming those 24 bits into a 128-bit hash code with the following properties.

Full Use of All Bits

A major strength of a computer-based encryption system like AES is the *key size*, the sheer number of possible keys facing an attacker. This strength disappears, however, if all the possible keys aren't actually being used. A good hash function must produce results across the full range of possible hash codes. Even for our short *dog* password, all 128 bits of the resulting hash code must be influenced by the original 24 bits of the password.

No Reversibility

In Chapter 1, you learned that an encryption method has to be reversible. A good hash function, in contrast, should *not* be reversible. I'll discuss why this is important later in the chapter. For now, know that for a given hash code, there should be no direct way to recover a password that produced it. I say *a* password and not *the* password because multiple passwords may produce the same hash code, which is known as a hash *collision*. Because there are more possible passwords than hash codes, collisions are inevitable. A good hash function should make it difficult for attackers to find *any* password that produces a given hash code.

Avalanche

The avalanche property that's vital to encryption is just as important in hashing. Small changes in the password should result in large changes in the hash code—especially since many people, when required to choose a new password, choose a slight variation of their old one. The hash code produced for *dog* should be very different from those produced by similar passwords such as *doge*, *Dog*, or *odg*.

The MD5 Hash Function

Meeting all these criteria is not easy. Good hash functions solve this problem in a clever way. They start with a jumble of bits and use the bit patterns of the password to modify this jumble further. That's the method of the widely used hash function called *MD5*—the fifth version of the *Message Digest* hash function.

Encoding the Password

To get started, MD5 converts the password to a 512-bit block; I'll call this the *encoded password*. The first part of this encoding consists of the ASCII codes of the characters in the password. For example, if the password is *BigFunTime*, the first character is a *B*, which has an ASCII byte of 01000010, so the first 8 bits of the encoded password are 01000010; the next 8 bits are the byte for *i*, which is 01101001; and so on. Thus, the 10 letters in our sample *BigFunTime* password will take up 80 bits out of 512.

Now the rest of the bits have to be filled up. The next bit is set to 1, and all the bits up to the last 64 are set to 0. The final 64 bits store a binary representation of the length, in bits, of the original password. In this case, the password is 10 characters, or 80 bits, long. The 64-bit binary representation of 80 is:

00000000 00000000 00000000 00000000 00000000 00000000 00000000 01010000

Clearly, we don't need 64 bits to store the length of a password. Using 64 bits for the length allows MD5 to hash inputs of arbitrary length—the benefit of which we'll see later.

Figure 2-1 shows the encoding of the sample password, organized into 16 numbered rows of 32 bits each.

```
1   01000010 01101001 01100111 01000110    Binary ASCII of
2   01110101 01101110 01010100 01101001    Password Letters
3   01101101 01100101 10000000 00000000
4   00000000 00000000 00000000 00000000
5   00000000 00000000 00000000 00000000
6   00000000 00000000 00000000 00000000
7   00000000 00000000 00000000 00000000    Padding
8   00000000 00000000 00000000 00000000
9   00000000 00000000 00000000 00000000
10  00000000 00000000 00000000 00000000
11  00000000 00000000 00000000 00000000
12  00000000 00000000 00000000 00000000
13  00000000 00000000 00000000 00000000
14  00000000 00000000 00000000 00000000
15  00000000 00000000 00000000 00000000    Number of Bits
16  00000000 00000000 00000000 01010000    in Password
```

Figure 2-1: The password BigFunTime transformed into the 512 bits used as input to the MD5 hash function

This encoded password is full of zeros and therefore doesn't meet the "fully uses all the bits" property of a good function, but that's okay because this is not the hash code; it's just the starting point.

Bitwise Operations

The MD5 hash function uses a few operations I haven't discussed before. Let's go through these briefly.

Binary Addition

The first new operation is *binary addition*. Binary addition is much like the decimal addition you already know but with binary numbers. For example, the 32-bit representation of the number 5 is:

```
00000000 00000000 00000000 00000101
```

The 32-bit representation of 46 is:

```
00000000 00000000 00000000 00101110
```

If we add 5 and 46 together, the result is 51. Likewise, the addition of those two binary representations results in the binary representation of 51:

```
00000000 00000000 00000000 00110011
```

Unlike normal addition, though, where sometimes the result has more digits than the operands, in binary addition the number of bits is fixed. If the result of adding two 32-bit binary numbers is greater than 32 bits, we ignore the "carry" at the left side of the result and keep only the 32 bits on the right. It's like working with a cheap calculator that has just a two-digit display, so when you add 75 and 49, instead of displaying 124, it displays only the last two digits, 24.

Bitwise NOT

The next new operation is called "not," often written in all uppercase as *NOT*. As demonstrated in Figure 2-2, NOT "flips" all of the bits, replacing each 1 with a 0 and each 0 with a 1.

Figure 2-2: The bitwise NOT operation. All bits are inverted. The 1 bits are highlighted for clarity.

Bitwise OR

Up next is *OR*, sometimes called *inclusive-OR* to distinguish it from the exclusive-or (XOR) that you saw in Chapter 1. The OR operation lines up two binary numbers with the same number of bits. In each position of the resulting binary number, you get a 1 if there's a 1 in the first number *or* in the second number; otherwise, you get a 0, as shown in Figure 2-3.

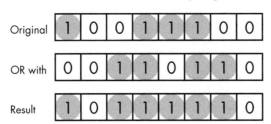

Figure 2-3: The bitwise OR operation. Bit positions are 1 in the result if they are 1 in either of the two inputs

Notice that unlike XOR, you can't apply OR twice and get the original byte back. It's a one-way trip.

Bitwise AND

The last of the new operations is *AND*. Two binary numbers are aligned, and in each position, the result is 1 wherever both bits are 1 in that position; otherwise, the result is 0. So a 1 in the result means there was a 1 in that position in the first number *and* the second number, as seen in Figure 2-4. As with OR, the AND operation isn't reversible.

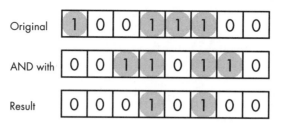

Figure 2-4: The bitwise AND operation. Bit positions are 1 in the result if they are 1 in both of the two inputs.

MD5 Hashing Rounds

Now we're ready for some hashing. Pieces of the encoded password make only brief appearances in the MD5 process, but those appearances make all the difference. The MD5 process always starts with the same 128 bits, conceptually split into four 32-bit sections, labeled A through D, as shown in Figure 2-5.

A   01100111 01000101 00100011 00000001

B   11101111 11001101 10101011 10001001

C   10011000 10111010 11011100 11111110

D   00010000 00110010 01010100 01110110

Figure 2-5: The starting configuration of the 128 bits of an MD5 hash code

From here, it's all about shifting these bits around and flipping them, in a process that repeats a whopping 64 times. In this respect, the process is a lot like AES but with even more rounds. Figure 2-6 is a broad diagram of one of the 64 rounds.

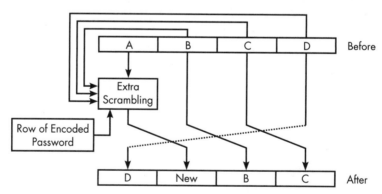

Figure 2-6: One round of the MD5 hash function. In the result, three of the sections are transposed, while all four sections are combined to make a new section.

As shown, sections B, C, and D are simply transposed, so that the D section of one round becomes the A section of the next. The main action of MD5 occurs in the "extra scrambling" of each round, which creates a new section from the bits of all four sections of the previous round. The extra scrambling uses the irreversible operations AND, OR, and NOT to combine the bits of all four sections with one of the rows of the encoded password. Different rows of the encoded password are used in different rounds, so that eventually all the rows of the encoded password are used multiple times. Because of the transposition, the process needs just four rounds to replace each of the four original sections with the result of the extra scrambling. After the complete 64-round process, the original bits of the sections will have been thoroughly sifted together with the encoded password.

Meeting the Criteria of a Good Hash Function

Because MD5 starts with an assortment of bits, then alters these bits over and over, adding in pieces of the encoded password, we can be sure that all the bits are affected along the way, giving us a true 128-bit hash code. The sheer number of operations that are irreversible—and remember, the actions described occur 64 times—means the hash function as a whole is not reversible. This rotation and alteration of the bits in the "extra scram- bling" each round, combined with the rotation of the sections themselves, distribute the bits and bytes and create the desired avalanche.

MD5 meets all the baseline requirements for a good hash function. It does have a few subtle weaknesses, however, as you'll soon see.

Digital Signatures

Hash functions serve other purposes in security besides creating keys from passwords. One of the most important is the creation of file *signatures*. As stated earlier, MD5 can process any size of input. If the input is larger than 512 bits, it's first divided into multiple 512-bit blocks. The MD5 process is then applied once per block. The first block starts with the initial 128 bits and each subsequent block starts with the hash code produced by the previous block. In this way, we could run the entire text of this book, an audio file, a video, or any other digital file through the function and get a single 128-bit hash code in return. This hash code would become the file's signature.

Why does a file need a signature? Suppose you have decided to down- load FreeWrite, a (fictional) freeware word processor application. You're wary, though, because of a bad experience in which you downloaded a free- ware program that turned out to be bogus and riddled with malware. To avoid this, you want to be sure the FreeWrite file that you download is the same file that the developers uploaded. The developers could hash the file with MD5 and post the resulting hash code—the file signature—on their website, freewrite.com. This allows you to run the file through an MD5 hash program and compare the result to the code on the developer site. If the new result doesn't match the signature, something has changed: the file, the signature, or both.

The Problem of Identity

Unfortunately, matching the posted hash code proves the FreeWrite file is legitimate only if the hash code was actually published by the developers. But what if an attacker copies the developer's freewrite.com site to a similarly named domain like free-write.com, and then posts a compromised file along with the hash of that compromised file? A digital signature is only as trustworthy as its provider. We'll explore this problem in further detail in Chapter 3.

Collision Attacks

Even with a matching hash code from a legitimate source, though, a file might be trouble. Many different files will produce the same hash code, which means an attacker trying to modify a file for nefarious purposes can avoid detection if the new, modified file produces the same hash code.

It's not too difficult to produce two files with the same hash code, which is known as a *collision attack*: just randomly generate files until two hash codes match. Finding a second file to match the *particular* hash code of another file is much harder. To be of any real use to an attacker, the file with the matching code can't be a bunch of random bytes; it has to be a program that does something malicious on the attacker's behalf.

Unfortunately, there are methods to produce a second file with the same MD5 code that is very similar to the first file. The discovery of this flaw in the MD5 hash function has led researchers to suggest that other hash functions be used for signatures. These more advanced hash functions usually have longer hash codes (up to 512 bits), more hashing rounds, and more complicated binary math during each round. As with encryption, though, there are no guarantees that flaws won't be discovered in the more complicated hash functions as well. Proper use of signatures means staying one step ahead of known design flaws because attackers will exploit flaws mercilessly. Digital security is a cat-and-mouse game in which the good guys are the mice, trying to avoid being eaten, never able to defeat the cats, and only hoping to stay alive a little longer.

Passwords in Authentication Systems

Nowhere is this cat-and-mouse game more evident than in authentication systems. Every place where you enter your password has to have a list of passwords to compare against, and properly securing the list requires great care.

The Dangers of Password Tables

Let's look at the most straightforward way passwords could be stored in a table. In this example, Northeast Money Bank (NEMB) stores the username and password of each of its customers, along with the account number and current balance. An excerpt from the password table is shown in Table 2-1.

Table 2-1: Poorly Designed Password Table

Username	Password	Account number	Balance
richguy22	ilikemoney	21647365	$27.21
mrgutman	falcon	32846519	$10,000.00
squire	yes90125	70023193	$145,398.44
burgomeister78	taco999	74766333	$732.23

Just as Kerckhoffs's principle says we can't rely on encryption methods remaining secret, we shouldn't rely on the password list remaining a secret, either. A disgruntled employee in the NEMB information technology department might easily acquire the file containing the list, or determined attackers on the outside might worm their way through the company defenses.

This is what's known as a *single point of defense*, meaning that once anyone lays eyes on this table, the game is over. First, this table shows the account numbers and balances of all of the customers, so at the very least, that's a major loss of privacy. What's even worse is that each password is stored in the form entered by the user. Accessing this password list will allow attackers to log on as any customer—a disaster in the making.

Fortunately, the problems with this storage system are easily remedied. Knowing that, and knowing how dangerous the system is, you would think that it would never be used. Sadly, you would be wrong. Real companies are storing user passwords just like this. Some extremely large companies that probably spent a great deal of money on their websites have been caught following this practice.

Hashing Passwords

If Table 2-1 shows the wrong thing to do, what's the right thing to do? One improvement is leaving the password out of the table and instead storing the hash code of the password, as shown by Table 2-2. (In the examples that follow, I show hash codes as decimal numbers to keep their length manageable.)

Table 2-2: Password Table with Hashed Passwords

Username	Hash of password	Account number	Balance
richguy22	330,711,060,038,684,200,901, 827,278,633,002,791,087	21647365	$27.21
mrgutman	332,375,033,828,033,552,423, 319,316,163,101,084,850	32846519	$10,000.00
squire	295,149,488,455,763,164,542, 524,060,437,757,020,453	70023193	$145,398.44
burgomeister78	133,039,589,388,270,767,475, 032,770,360,311,206,892	74766333	$732.23

When a user tries to log in, the submitted password is hashed and the result compared to the stored hash code. If they match, the user is logged in. Because the hash function isn't reversible, getting access to the table isn't the same as getting access to the passwords. An attacker can't log on to an account with the hash code.

The account number and balance are still stored as plaintext, though, and it would be a good idea to encrypt them, making a table with only hash codes and ciphertext. The problem is if we used the hash of the password as our cipher key, then encrypting the data provides no additional protection because anyone who acquires this table will be able to decrypt the ciphertext.

There are several ways to solve this problem. One solution is to use one hash function to transform the password for authentication and another hash function to transform the password into a cipher key to encrypt the account number and balance. As long as the hash functions are not reversible, this solution would provide security for the account data even if an attacker got access to the table.

Dictionary Attacks

Hashing the passwords is a good defense against attackers, but it's not enough. Authentication systems are still vulnerable to *dictionary attacks*.

In a basic dictionary attack, the attacker has no access to the password table and must guess the password. The attacker could just try random jumbles of characters but will have much more success with a *dictionary*, which in the world of software is simply a list of words. In this case, the dictionary is a list of the most common passwords, and it begins something like this:

- password
- 123456
- football
- mypassword
- abcdef

To foil the basic dictionary attack, most sites count the number of failed logins and, after a certain number (perhaps as few as three), temporarily prevent further login attempts from a particular computer. This renders the attack impractical by increasing the time required to find the right password.

A different form of dictionary attack is used when an attacker has acquired a copy of a hashed and encrypted password table. In this case, the attacker hashes each password in the dictionary and compares it to each of the hash codes in the stolen table. When a match is discovered, the attacker knows the password that generates that user's hash code. To save time, the attacker can run all the passwords in the dictionary through a selected hash function once and store the results in a dictionary like in Table 2-3.

Table 2-3: Dictionary with Hash Codes

Password	MD5 hash code
password	126,680,608,771,750,945,340,162,210,354,335,764,377
123456	299,132,688,689,127,175,738,334,524,183,350,839,358
football	74,046,754,153,250,065,911,729,167,268,259,247,040
mypassword	69,792,856,232,803,413,714,004,936,714,872,372,804
abcdef	308,439,634,705,511,765,949,277,356,614,095,247,246

Dictionaries demonstrate why it is important for users to choose passwords that aren't obvious. The more obscure a password, the less likely it will be in an attacker's dictionary.

Hash Tables

Unfortunately, an attacker can dispense with the dictionary altogether and build a table of randomly generated passwords and their corresponding hash codes, which I'll call a *precomputed hash table*. Of course, the number of potential passwords is enormous, so if the attacker wants a decent chance of getting a match, the hash table needs to be huge. Building a precomputed hash table takes a lot of computing power and time, but it only has to be built once, and then it can be used over and over again.

One weakness of the table is that its sheer size can make searching for a match extremely slow. When you consider how fast a word processor can find a particular word in a large document, this may seem surprising, but these precomputed tables are much larger than any file on your computer. Suppose an attacker has a table of all passwords composed of 10 or fewer uppercase and lowercase letters and digits. Even with these restrictions, the number of potential passwords is 62^{10}, which is 839,299,365,868,340,224. The precomputed hash table won't need every one of these potential passwords as entries, but it would need to have a sizable fraction. The table would be so large, though, it couldn't fit in a computer's internal memory. It couldn't even fit on a hard drive—or just to get to the point, it's so big it might need to be split across a million hard drives. And that's just the storage problem. Unless you have the distributed computing power of Google, it's not practical to search a table that large. (And searching a huge mass of data isn't easy even for Google; we'll explore searching in detail in Chapter 7.)

Hash Chaining

Because a precomputed hash table is too large to store and search, attackers use a clever technique called *hash chaining* to drastically reduce the number of entries in the table without reducing its effectiveness. This technique uses a different type of function called a *reduction function* that does the same sorts of mathematical gyrations as a hash function but with the opposite purpose. Instead of creating a hash code from a password, it creates a password from a hash code—not the password that produced the hash, but simply a sequence of characters with the form of a valid password.

Here's an example of hash chaining. When *glopp26taz* is hashed using MD5, it produces this hash code:

$$22,964,925,579,257,552,835,515,378,304,344,866,835$$

A reduction function transforms this hash code into another valid password, say, *7HGupp2tss*. This, in turn, is sent through the hash function, producing another hash code, which is sent through the reduction function to generate another password, and so on. An alternating series of passwords and hash codes, such as that shown in Figure 2-7, is a *hash chain*.

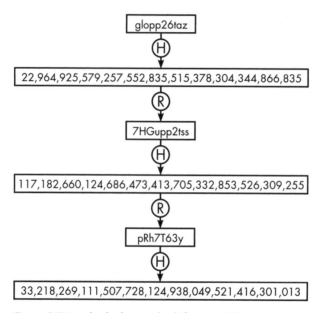

Figure 2-7: In a hash chain, a hash function (H) alternates with a reduction function (R) that produces an arbitrary password from a hash code.

Instead of a table of passwords and hash codes, the attacker generates a series of hash chains, each of the same length, storing only the first and last links of each chain. The chain in Figure 2-7 is shown as the third entry in Table 2-4. This table has 5 entries, but each entry is a chain of 3 password/hash pairs, making this the equivalent of a plain table of 15 entries.

Table 2-4: Hash Chain Table

Start	End
sop3H4Yzai	302,796,960,148,170,554,741,517,711,430,674,339,836
5jhfHTeu4y	333,226,570,587,833,594,170,987,787,116,324,792,461
glopp26taz	33,218,269,111,507,728,124,938,049,521,416,301,013
YYhs9j2a22	145,483,602,575,738,705,325,298,600,400,764,586,970
Pr2u912mn1	737,08,819,301,203,417,973,443,363,267,460,459,460

Figure 2-8 shows an example of using the table. Our attacker is trying to recover the password for the target hash code 117,182,660,124,686,473, 413,705,332,853,526,309,255. The attacker must determine which chain in the table, if any, contains the target hash code. First, the target code is compared against every number in the End column of the table. In this case, no match is found, so the attacker runs the target hash code through the reduction function to make a new password, runs that result through the hashing function, and then searches for this new hash code in the End column of the table. This process will continue until a match is found, or after the process is run three times (the length of the chains in this table).

In this case, the initial target hash value is reduced to the password *pRh7T63y*, which, in turn, is hashed, and this new hash value appears in the third entry of the table, in the chain with the starting password *glopp26taz*. That identifies the hash chain in which the target password may appear, but the attacker must obtain the password by iterating through this chain. The starting password in that chain is hashed; the resulting hash value is not a match for the initial hash value, so it is reduced to a new password, *7HGupp2tss*, and hashed again. This hash code *does* match, which means *7HGupp2tss* is the password.

Hash code chains dramatically shrink the table while still providing the same amount of searchable data. For example, if a chain has 100 passwords and 100 hash codes, then the password matching any of those hash codes can be indirectly retrieved using that chain, even though the chain has only one password and hash code in the table. Therefore, a table with chains that long has the power of a regular precomputed hash table 100 times larger.

There are some potential snags, though. For one, searching takes more computational effort with hash chains. Also, because of collisions—multiple passwords that produce the same hash code—a matching chain doesn't necessarily contain the searched-for hash code and its matching password, a problem known as *chain merging*. These are small consolations for those of us worried about our data security, however. There are methods for reducing the chain merging problem, but even without them, it's clear that effective precomputed tables can be made for particular hash functions, rendering the passwords that use them vulnerable.

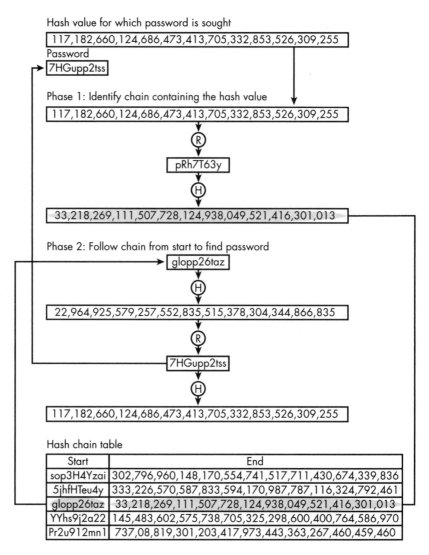

Hash value for which password is sought
| 117,182,660,124,686,473,413,705,332,853,526,309,255 |

Password
| 7HGupp2tss |

Phase 1: Identify chain containing the hash value
| 117,182,660,124,686,473,413,705,332,853,526,309,255 |

(R)

| pRh7T63y |

(H)

| 33,218,269,111,507,728,124,938,049,521,416,301,013 |

Phase 2: Follow chain from start to find password
| glopp26taz |

(H)

| 22,964,925,579,257,552,835,515,378,304,344,866,835 |

(R)

| 7HGupp2tss |

(H)

| 117,182,660,124,686,473,413,705,332,853,526,309,255 |

Hash chain table

Start	End
sop3H4Yzai	302,796,960,148,170,554,741,517,711,430,674,339,836
5jhfHTeu4y	333,226,570,587,833,594,170,987,787,116,324,792,461
glopp26taz	33,218,269,111,507,728,124,938,049,521,416,301,013
YYhs9j2a22	145,483,602,575,738,705,325,298,600,400,764,586,970
Pr2u912mn1	737,08,819,301,203,417,973,443,363,267,460,459,460

Figure 2-8: Using a hash chain table to find a password that produces a particular hash code. Neither the password nor the hash code is listed in the table.

Iterative Hashing

One way to thwart the creation of precomputed hash tables is to apply the hash function more than once. Because the output of a hash function can itself be hashed, the original password can pass through the same hash function any number of times. This technique, unhelpfully, is also known as *hash chaining*, but to avoid confusion, I will refer to it as *iterative hashing*. Figure 2-9 shows a five-deep iterative hashing of the password *football*.

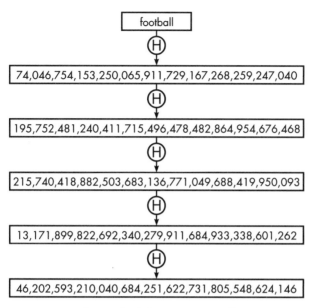

Figure 2-9: Applying a hash function repeatedly

With this technique, passwords are repeatedly hashed when the password is stored and when the user logs in. To thwart this, the attacker has to produce a table based on the same idea, running the chosen hash code function the same number of times. From Kerchkoffs's principle, we know that cryptographic systems shouldn't depend on keeping their methods secret. The goal of iterative hashing isn't to disguise how many times the password is hashed, but to make the creation of the attacker's precomputed hash table as difficult as possible. In the example, the password runs through the hash function five times. That would multiply the time needed to create the attacker's table by five as well. In real-world use, passwords can be run through hash functions hundreds or thousands of times. Is this enough to prevent the creation of useful precomputed hash tables? Maybe. Computers get faster every day. For the most part, this is wonderful, but the downside to ever-increasing computational power is that it keeps pushing the boundary of practical limitations, and so much of our information security is based on these practical limitations.

Someone setting up a password system based on iterative hashing has to choose the number of iterations. It's fairly easy to choose a number that provides good security today. What's difficult is predicting the number of iterations required a year from now, or 2 years, or 10.

You might think the best choice is some impossibly large number to guard against the power of future computers. The problem is that today's computers would have real trouble processing legitimate logins. Would you be willing to wait five minutes to access one of your online accounts?

Salting Passwords

Authentication systems need a way to strengthen hashing without a performance-crushing number of hash iterations; that is, they need a method of storing passwords that requires an impractical time investment from attackers without creating an equally unrealistic time burden on legitimate access. That method is called *salt*. Salt is an apt term for this concept, and I commend whoever came up with it. In culinary usage, a pinch of salt profoundly changes the flavor of a dish. In cryptography, a small quantity of salt sprinkled on a password dramatically changes its hash code.

Here's how it works: when a new user signs up for an account and selects a username and password, the system automatically generates the salt for that account. The salt is a string of characters, like a short, random password, that is combined with the user's password before hashing. For example, user *mrgutman* chooses *falcon* as his password, and the system generates *h38T2* as the salt.

The salt and password can be combined in various ways, but the simplest is appending the salt to the end of the password, resulting in *falconh38T2* in this example. This combination is then hashed, and the hash code stored in the authentication table along with the username and the salt, as shown in Table 2-5.

Table 2-5: Password Table Using Salt

Username	Salt	Hash of password + salt
richguy22	7Pmnq	106,736,954,704,360,738,602,545,963,558, 770,944,412
mrgutman	h38T2	142,858,562,082,404,032,402,440,010,972, 328,251,653
squire	93ndy	122,446,997,766,728,224,659,318,737,810, 478,984,316
burgomeister78	HuOw2	64,383,697,378,169,783,622,186,691,431, 070,835,777

Each time a user requests access, the salt is added to the end of the entered password before hashing. An attacker who acquires a copy of this authentication table can't get much use out of a precomputed hash table. Although the table might have a password that hashes to the given code, that password won't produce the right code when combined with the salt. Instead, the attacker would need to create a table for a specific salt. That could be done, but remember that the salt is randomly chosen. If there are, say, 100,000 users in a stolen authentication table, and the salts are numerous enough that no salt is duplicated in the table, the attacker will need to create 100,000 tables. At this point, we can't even call them precomputed tables because the attacker is creating them for each attack.

Are Password Tables Safe?

Salting and iterative hashing are typically used together, creating real head-aches for an attacker. Iterative hashing increases the time requirement for creating a single precomputed hash table, and salting means an attacker has to make a multitude of tables. But is this combination enough?

There is no definitive answer to that question. Cryptography researchers and security experts continue to develop new defenses against unauthorized access. At the same time, though, attackers continue to find new methods to penetrate defenses. Advances in computational power and programming theory help whichever side takes advantage of them first.

Perhaps the most important lesson of this discussion is that security is often out of the user's hands. There will always be vulnerabilities, but there's no way for a user to know if a particular site or service is employing the best security practices. The salt technique, for example, benefits only systems that use it, and not every system does.

Password Storage Services

That's how passwords are stored on remote authentication systems. What about on the user end? How do we safely store our passwords?

A long time ago, I had so few passwords that I could safely entrust them to my memory, but eventually I knew I had to store passwords outside of my head. Writing the passwords on a piece of paper, though, is just a different kind of security liability. For a while, I had an elaborate homebrew solution involving a *.txt* file encrypted with AES and stored on a memory card that was kept in a metal box that was probably not 100 percent fireproof. This arrange-ment worked, except that every time I needed to look up a password, I had to go to the box, get the memory card, slot it into my computer, double-click the file, type the password (the one password I had to remember), and find the desired entry in my table.

Eventually I threw in the towel and signed up for a web-based pass-word storage service. When I created an account with the service, I chose a master password. I then stored all my other passwords and usernames on this website. This information is stored in a way that renders it of little use to anyone who gains access to the raw data, so if my password at Amazon is *chickenfat* (it isn't), then the word *chickenfat* isn't stored anywhere on the password storage server. Instead, the passwords are encrypted by a program on my browser before being sent to the password storage site, using my cho-sen master password to generate the encryption key. Therefore, even if the server were breached, the attacker wouldn't be able to retrieve my individ-ual passwords without the master password.

The master password itself is not stored on the password storage site, either. When the encryption key is needed to encrypt or decrypt an indi-vidual login, the master password is salted and then hashed repeatedly, for as many iterations as I specify.

Although using a password storage service puts all of my eggs in one basket, so to speak, this frees me to use best practices for individual logins. Whereas previously I might have created passwords that were collages of words and numbers I thought I could remember, now my passwords are lengthy random jumbles. And they are all different because I no longer need to remember them all.

A Final Thought

In all of this talk about authentication systems, I've avoided a crucial detail. Authentication systems compare stored user passwords to passwords provided during logons, but how does the remote computer doing the authentication get the users' chosen passwords in the first place? Secure transmission requires encryption, which implies the users would have had to encrypt the passwords—but how could the remote system decrypt the encrypted passwords without having the passwords already? This brings us back to the shared key problem—none of what we talked about in this chapter can work unless that problem is solved. So that's what we'll do next.

3

WEB SECURITY

You may not have realized it before, but the Internet as we know it couldn't exist without a solution to the shared key problem. Think about a typical situation: you're buying something at an online retailer that you've never purchased from before. At some point you will be asked for your credit card data. Your browser tells you that your data is secure, perhaps by displaying a "lock" icon in the corner. But for the browser to protect your card number using AES, both your system and the retailer must use the same encryption key. How do two systems securely transmit data without getting together beforehand to exchange a key?

Solving this shared key problem is essential to providing any security on the Web. We'll explore the solution to the shared key problem in this chapter, which uses all the techniques we've seen in the previous two chapters, plus a new special ingredient: public-key cryptography.

How Public-Key Cryptography Solves the Shared Key Problem

In the world of physical security, the shared key problem has a straightforward solution because locks and keys are two separate things. Suppose person A needs to ship confidential physical documents to person B. Person B could buy a strongbox and a keyed lock and then mail the box and lock to person A while keeping the key. Then person A puts the documents in the box, locks the box with B's lock, and ships the box back to B. Because B has the only key to the lock, this is a secure delivery method.

This is the desired situation for transmitting data digitally as well. We need to separate the methods for locking and unlocking data, so that knowing how to encrypt data won't provide the means to decrypt the resulting ciphertext.

In Chapter 1, we learned about AES, which is a symmetric-key encryption method, meaning the same key is used for encryption and decryption. For transmission, we need an *asymmetric-key* encryption method, with one key for encryption and another key for decryption. The encryption key is known as the *public key*, because it can be freely distributed with no ill effects if it falls into the hands of an attacker; for this reason, asymmetric-key encryption is also known as *public-key cryptography*. The decryption key is known only to the recipient, so it's known as the *private key*. These relationships are shown in Figure 3-1.

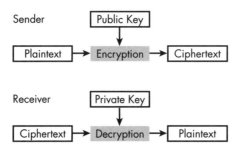

Figure 3-1: Asymmetric-key encryption, with a public key for encryption and a private key for decryption. Only the receiver has the private key.

Math Tools for Public-Key Cryptography

What public-key cryptography requires, then, is an encryption method that's reversible but *not* with the cipher key that was used in the encryption. The basic tools of the encryption methods we've seen so far won't work for public-key cryptography. The most common operation in AES, for example, is exclusive-or, which is used precisely because when something is XORed twice with the same binary number, you get the same number you started with. Reversible operations such as XOR inevitably lead to having the same key for encryption and decryption.

Public-key encryption, therefore, requires a new technique. As it turns out, the secrets to public-key encryption lie in the hidden relationships between numbers. In order to explain what those relationships are and how they can be exploited for cryptography, we need to go over a few pieces of math terminology.

Invertible Functions

Broadly stated, a *function* describes any situation where each numerical input results in a single numerical output. The current Celsius temperature, for example, is a function of the current Fahrenheit temperature. For any particular temperature in Fahrenheit degrees, there is exactly one matching temperature in Celsius degrees.

In the same way, the monetary value of a pile of coins is a function of the number of coins of each type. A pile containing three quarters, two nickels, a dime, and four pennies has a monetary value of 99 cents. This pile of coins cannot be worth any other amount.

Sometimes a function can be reversed to produce another function. If we know a temperature in degrees Fahrenheit, we also know it in degrees Celsius, and the reverse is true: if we know a temperature in Celsius, we can also figure it out in Fahrenheit. In mathematical terms, we would say that the Celsius-to-Fahrenheit function is the *inversion* of the Fahrenheit-to-Celsius function, and that the original function is *invertible*. The coin example, though, is not invertible. The same total monetary value can be produced by multiple combinations of coins. If the coins in my pocket are worth 99 cents, I might have three quarters, two nickels, a dime, and four pennies, or I might have nine dimes and nine pennies, or some other combination.

One-Way Functions

For some invertible functions, computing in one direction may be a lot easier than the other. For example, the mathematical concepts of *square* and *square root* are complementary functions. Suppose you have a square room in your home that is covered in black-and-white tiles, as shown in Figure 3-2. To find the total surface area of the floor, you multiply 12 by 12 to get 144.

We say that 144 is the *square* of 12. Going in the other direction, we say that 12 is the *square root* of 144. These are both functions; each number has one square and one square root. The difficulty of computing these two functions is very different, though. Figuring out a number's square is easy: you just multiply the number by itself. Figuring out the square root is hard. Unless you have a table of values to help you, computing a square root is effectively a trial-and-error process. You make a guess at what the root might be, multiply that guess by itself, see if your guess was too high or too low, and then adjust your next guess accordingly, repeating the process until you find the exact square root or get close enough that you are willing to stop. When a function is invertible but its inverse is much harder to compute, it is called a *one-way function*.

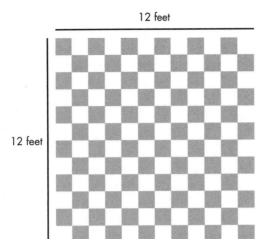

12 feet

12 feet

Figure 3-2: A square room with walls 12 feet long has a total area of 144 feet.

Trapdoor Functions

Asymmetric encryption requires a one-way function so that the encryption key can be public—the encryption will be easy, but the decryption will be so hard as to be infeasible. The problem is, we shouldn't make the decryption infeasible for the intended recipient as well. So any old one-way function isn't going to do the trick. We need what's known as a *trapdoor function*, a one-way function where the inverse function is hard in general, but easy when some secret value is known.

Prime Numbers

The particular trapdoor function we'll discuss involves prime numbers. A number is *prime* if it is greater than 1 and can only be divided (without a remainder) by itself and 1. For example, 5 is prime because it can be divided only by itself and 1. It cannot be evenly divided into 2, 3, or 4 parts. The number 6, though, can be divided by 2 and 3 in addition to 1 and itself. It is therefore a nonprime, or *composite*, number. Smaller numbers that divide into a larger number are known as the larger number's *factors*. Every number is divisible by itself and by 1, but we call these *trivial factors* and tend to ignore them when discussing factors. A prime number has only trivial factors.

Coprime Numbers

In a related concept, two numbers are said to be *coprime* if they share only 1 as a factor. Either number may or may not be prime itself, but each can be thought of as prime as far as the other number knows. For example, the composite numbers 9 and 4 are coprime because there is no number that divides them both except for 1. In contrast, 6 isn't coprime with either 9 or 4, because 6 shares factors with both. These relationships are demonstrated in Table 3-1.

Table 3-1: Showing that 9 and 4 Are Coprime, but 6 Is Not Coprime with 9 or 4

Divisor	Remainder from 9	Remainder from 6	Remainder from 4
9	(trivial)		
8	1		
7	2		
6	3	(trivial)	
5	4	1	
4	1	2	(trivial)
3	0	0	1
2	1	0	0
1	(trivial)	(trivial)	(trivial)

Although 1 is not a prime number, it's considered to be coprime with every other number.

Prime Factors

Now we are getting close to the hidden relationships that make public-key encryption work. If we multiply two prime numbers, the resulting product has only those two prime numbers as factors (again, not counting itself and 1). For example, 5 and 3 are prime numbers. The product of 3 and 5 is 15, and 15 has only 3 and 5 as factors, as shown in Table 3-2.

Table 3-2: The Product of Prime Numbers 3 and 5 Is 15, and 15 Has Only 3 and 5 as Factors

Divide 15 by	Result	Remainder
15	0	0 (trivial)
14	1	1
13	1	2
12	1	3
11	1	4
10	1	5
9	1	6
8	1	7
7	2	1
6	2	3
5	3	0
4	3	3
3	5	0
2	7	1
1	15	0 (trivial)

This is a one-way function. If I give you two prime numbers, you can easily multiply them together, although you might use a calculator if the numbers are large. The inverse of this function would mean starting with the product of two prime numbers and finding the two original primes. That's considerably harder.

Let's take 18,467 as an example. This number is indeed the product of two primes—but *which* two primes? To answer this question, you would need to divide 18,467 by every prime number starting from 2. Eventually you would discover that 18,467 divided by 59 is 313, which means that 59 and 313 are the two prime factors.

Finding the prime factors is very difficult if all you have is the product. However, when you have the product and one of the two factors, finding the other factor is simple, because all you have to do is divide the first prime into the product. That makes it a trapdoor function—easy in one direction, hard in another unless you have the extra piece of information. If the prime numbers are large enough, finding the factors is infeasible without the trapdoor.

The RSA Encryption Method

This trapdoor function is at the heart of the *RSA* public-key encryption system, named after the initials of its inventors: Rivest, Shamir, and Adleman. In actual practice, this system uses very large numbers to prevent a simple brute-force attack, but I'll use small numbers in a simplified example to more easily demonstrate how it works.

Suppose that siblings Zed and Abigail share a bank account but live apart. Zed has just changed the account's four-digit PIN to 1482 and needs to send this new number to Abigail via email. Because email transmissions pass through many potentially insecure computers, the PIN must be encrypted in some way, but Zed and Abigail haven't previously shared a cipher key that would allow the use of a method like AES. Instead, Zed will securely transmit the new PIN using RSA.

Creating the Keys

Although Zed has the confidential data to transmit in this example, the RSA procedure begins with Abigail, who must produce a public key before Zed can encrypt the PIN.

Step 1

Abigail begins by choosing two prime numbers; let's say she chooses 97 and 113.

Step 2

Abigail multiplies these two numbers together to get 10,961. To keep things straight, I'll call this number the *prime-product*.

Step 3

Next Abigail must compute a *totient* (which is pronounced *TOE-shent*, to rhyme with *quotient*). For a number *N*, the totient is the amount of numbers that are less than *N* and coprime with *N*. For example, the number 15 is coprime with 1, 2, 4, 7, 8, 11, 13, or 14, as shown in Figure 3-3. Because there are eight numbers coprime with 15, the totient of 15 is 8.

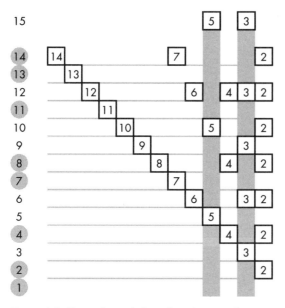

Figure 3-3: The eight circled numbers have no factors in common with 15. Therefore the totient of 15 is 8.

Computing the totient of a number normally requires checking every smaller number for common factors, and therefore it's a lot of work—for huge numbers, finding the totient is practically impossible. However, if the number in question is the product of two prime numbers, there's a shortcut: simply subtract 1 from each of the two prime numbers and multiply the results together. For example, 15 is the product of two primes, 3 and 5. If we subtract 1 from each of the two primes, we get 2 and 4; if we multiply 2 and 4 we get 8, the totient of 15.

This shortcut greatly aids Abigail, whose next step is computing the totient of the prime-product, 10,961. Since that is the product of the primes 97 and 113, the totient of 10,961 is 96 × 112, or 10,752.

Step 4

Now Abigail selects a number that meets the following criteria:

- Greater than 1
- Less than the totient
- Coprime with the totient

Let's say she picks 5. This is acceptable because it is greater than 1, it is less than 10,752, and there is no number other than 1 that divides both 5 and 10,752. Abigail is going to share this number with Zed, so we'll call it the public key.

Step 5

The chosen public key determines Abigail's private key, the number she has to keep secret. For any given public key and totient, there is just one number that can serve as the private key, and we can identify it by testing successive multiples of the totient. For each multiple, we add 1 and see if the result is divisible by the public key. When it is, the result of this division is the private key.

The process is demonstrated in Table 3-3. The first multiple of 10,752 is 10,752 itself; Abigail adds 1 to make 10,753, then divides by 5, getting 2,150 with a remainder of 3. She tries the second multiple, 21,504, and when she adds 1 and divides by 5, she gets 4,301 and no remainder, so her private key is 4,301.

Table 3-3: Finding the Private Key

Multiple	Multiply by 10,752	Add 1	Divide by 5	Remainder
1	10,752	10,753	2,150	3
2	21,504	21,505	4,301	0

Of course, with larger numbers it may take a lot more multiples to find the private key, but there is always one number that will pass the test. The number of multiples tested will always be less than the public key (in our example, Abigail knows she'll find the private key in four tries or less). In any case, now that Abigail has her private key, the actual encryption can begin.

Encrypting Data with RSA

Abigail emails both her prime-product (10,961) and public key (5) to Zed. Because these numbers don't allow anyone to decrypt the resulting cipher-text, it doesn't matter who else reads the email before it reaches Zed.

The actual encryption of the new PIN takes just two steps.

Step 1

Zed raises the PIN, 1,482, to the power of the public key, 5—that is, 1,482 is multiplied by itself five times:

$$1{,}482 \times 1{,}482 \times 1{,}482 \times 1{,}482 \times 1{,}482 = 7{,}148{,}929{,}565{,}430{,}432$$

Step 2

The second step is to find the remainder of dividing the result of step 1 by the prime-product. In this case, 10,961 goes into 7,148,929,565,430,432 about 652 billion times, but all Zed cares about is that the remainder of that division is 2,122. Zed sends this remainder to Abigail.

Step 3

On the receiving end, Abigail performs two similar steps to decrypt the ciphertext. She starts by raising the ciphertext number, 2,122, to the power of the private key, 4,301. Because $2,122^{4,301}$ is enormous—over 14,000 digits—I won't show it here.

Step 4

Abigail finds the remainder of dividing the enormous number from step 3 by the prime-product. The remainder of that division is exactly 1,482, revealing Zed's PIN.

RSA Effectiveness

Remember that the goal of RSA, like any encryption system, is making encryption easy, decryption easy for the intended recipient, and decryption very hard for anyone else. A summary of our RSA example is shown in Figure 3-4.

Even using much larger primes, encryption and authorized decryption are easy with the aid of the computer, as a review of the steps in our example will show.

1. Abigail picked two prime numbers and multiplied them together to produce her *prime-product*. Multiplying two numbers together is easy.

2. Abigail computed the *totient* of the prime-product by subtracting one from each of the two prime numbers before multiplying. Subtraction and multiplication are easy.

3. Abigail chose a *public key*, a number that shares no factors with the totient. For large numbers, this would be impractical to find by hand, but for a computer, this is easy.

4. Abigail found the appropriate value for her *private key*, which should, when multiplied by the number chosen for her public key, produce a number that's 1 more than a multiple of the totient. This is a chore to do by hand, but for a computer, this too is easy.

5. Abigail sent Zed the prime-product and public key.

6. Zed raised the PIN to the power of the public key. For a computer, this is relatively easy.

7. Zed divided the result from the previous step by the prime-product and took the remainder. Division is easy.

8. Zed sent the remainder to Abigail.

9. Abigail raised the number Zed sent to the power of the private key. Easy.

10. Abigail divided the result of the previous step by the prime-product and took the remainder, revealing Zed's PIN. Easy.

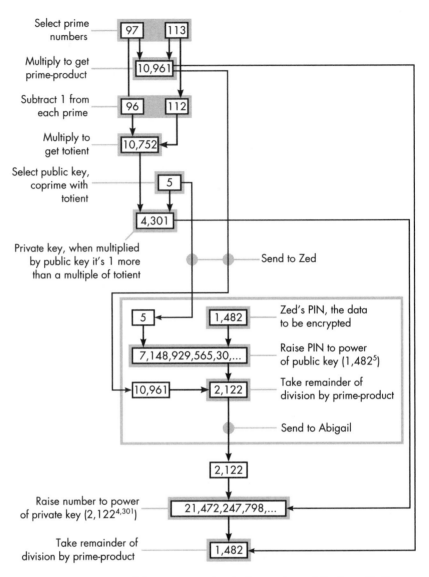

Figure 3-4: A summary of the RSA example. The box in the middle shows Zed's responsibilities; the rest are Abigail's.

RSA encryption and decryption by authorized parties is easy work for a computer, but unauthorized decryption is maddeningly difficult. To decrypt, an attacker must have both the prime-product, which Abigail gives out freely, and the private key, which she keeps to herself. How could an attacker compute the private key? Finding that number means first finding the totient of the prime-product, but remember, Abigail was only able to compute the totient quickly because she knows the two prime numbers that created the prime-product. Without those two prime numbers, an attacker must find the totient the hard way—by checking every number less than the prime-product to find all the coprimes.

In our example, the prime-product is small, so it's feasible for a computer to find the totient in this brute-force manner. In actual practice, though, prime-products are huge, and finding their totients isn't feasible at all. In fact, an attacker would be better off searching for the two primes that make the prime-product, to use the shortcut method of making the totient. That still requires checking all numbers up to the square root of the prime-product, though, so for large numbers this is as infeasible as finding the totient the long way.

The RSA encryption method therefore creates our desired digital equivalent of a "lockbox." Encryption and decryption no longer share the same secrets, so knowing how to lock the data doesn't provide the ability to unlock it.

RSA Use in the Real World

Our simplified example demonstrates the basics of RSA encryption, but for real-world use, we have to consider a few other details.

Bidirectional Transmission

The system shown in the example allows for Zed to securely transmit to Abigail, but not the other way around. If they wanted to send secure messages in either direction, Zed would have to go through all the steps that Abigail did, making his own prime-product, totient, public key, and private key, and sending the prime-product and public key to Abigail.

Key Size

In RSA, the last step of either encryption or decryption is taking the remainder of division with the prime-product, which means the plaintext number must be less than the prime-product. In the example with Abigail and Zed, then, the largest possible plaintext number is 14,960. That's not a problem for Zed and his four-digit PIN, but for general use larger ranges are needed.

Just as important, the larger the value of the prime-product, the more difficult it will be for an attacker to find the two prime factors. In other words, the size of the prime-product directly affects the security of encryption. In current practice, primes are chosen to produce a prime-product with a minimum of 1,024 bits. As you may recall, the Advanced Encryption Standard described in Chapter 1 used only 128 or 256 bits for the key. So we are talking about a truly humongous number—1,024 bits is equivalent to a decimal number of over 300 digits.

Long Plaintexts and Performance

A 1,024-bit key allows the encryption of very large numbers. But a typical text, image, or audio file is a long series of small numbers, not one big number. How do we transmit a long series of numbers using RSA? With AES, long files would be chopped up into as many 128-bit blocks as necessary.

In theory, we could do the same with RSA, chopping up files into a multitude of 1,024-bit blocks and applying RSA to each block. The problem is that RSA encryption is much slower than AES.

AES has more steps than the RSA Encryption Standard, but even so, AES is high-performance because the steps themselves are so simple. The most common operations are XOR and shifting bits around, and these operations are individually trivial. You can grasp this by working out the result of these operations in your head, as shown in Figure 3-5.

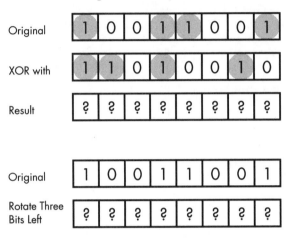

Figure 3-5: Computing XOR or rotating bits to new positions is easy.

In contrast, the RSA process has only a few steps, but the reliance on exponentiation means more work overall. Consider a relatively small exponent: 17^{16}. Written out, that's . . .

$$17 \times 17 \times 17 \times 17 \times 17 \times 17 \times 17 \times 17 \times 17 \times 17 \times 17 \times 17 \times 17 \times 17 \times 17 \times 17$$

Try working that out in your head, and you see the problem. Now imagine exponents involving numbers with hundreds of digits. Although a computer can handle these calculations, exponents are clearly a lot more work than simple XORs. Because exponents take so much time, using RSA for large amounts of data is impractical.

Combining Systems

The solution to the RSA performance problem is simple: don't transmit large amounts of data with RSA. Instead, use RSA to transmit an encryption key for another, faster method, such as AES.

Returning to Abigail and Zed, suppose Zed needs to send Abigail a long document that he has already converted to a series of numbers using the ASCII table. Zed would prefer to encrypt the document using AES rather than take on the hard work of RSA. To use AES, though, Zed and Abigail would both need to share an AES encryption key. RSA provides the means to share that key safely. Zed can create the AES key himself, then encrypt it with RSA using Abigail's public key. Then Zed can encrypt the long document using AES, and Abigail can decrypt the resulting ciphertext using the key they now share. This process is illustrated in Figure 3-6.

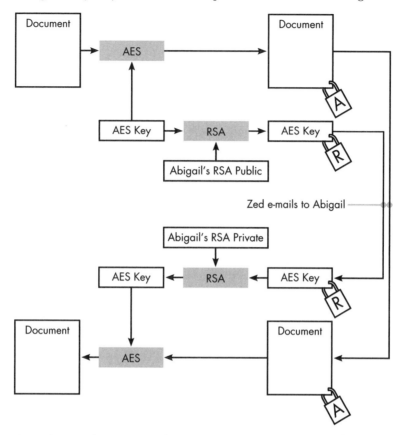

Figure 3-6: Combining RSA and AES to produce an asymmetric public-key system with high performance

In this figure, the A-lock symbol means "encrypted with AES" while the R-lock means "encrypted with RSA." By sending both the AES-encrypted document and the AES key encrypted with her public RSA key, Abigail has everything necessary to decrypt the document, but an attacker intercepting the transmission won't be able to decrypt the document without Abigail's private key.

By combining the two encryption methods, we combine their strengths to get the high performance of AES and the shared keys of RSA. Public-key encryption is typically used this way, to initiate a symmetric-key encryption process that would otherwise be impossible.

RSA for Authentication

Public-key cryptography creates an authentication problem. Because the public key is just that—public—anyone can send an encrypted message to the private key owner; therefore, the recipient of a transmission cannot be certain of the sender's identity. This problem doesn't occur with symmetric-key encryption, because the secrecy of the one key, when it can be shared, ensures not only the security of the message but also that the message originated with the other person who has the key. Luckily, public-key cryptography can be also be used to authenticate.

Authentication Using RSA

In our RSA example, Abigail has her prime-product of 10,961 and her private key of 4,301, while Zed has the prime-product and Abigail's public key of 5. This allows Zed to send a secure message to Abigail, but it also allows Abigail to send an authenticated message to Zed.

Suppose Abigail wants to send that same PIN, 1482, back to Zed to acknowledge its receipt, and in such a way that Zed can be sure the acknowledgment comes from Abigail.

Abigail takes the PIN, 1,482, and raises it to the power of her private key (instead of the public key used for encryption). $1,482^{4,301}$ is another huge number—it has over 13,000 digits—so I'm not going to write it here, but when that huge number is divided by the prime-product of 10,961, the remainder is 8,742. Abigail sends an email with that remainder to Zed. Zed now raises that 8,742 to the power of Abigail's public key, 5, which results in 51,056,849,256,616,667,232. Finally, Zed divides that number by the prime-product, getting a remainder of 1,482. Zed recognizes this number as the PIN, and knows it must have been transformed using Abigail's private key, proving the number came from Abigail. The relationship between security and authentication in RSA is shown in Figure 3-7.

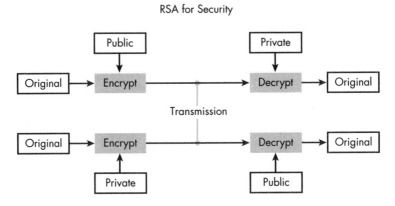

Figure 3-7: The RSA process provides either encryption or authentication.

We can authenticate entire files by applying this authentication process to the encryption key of a system like AES and sending the encrypted file and the authenticated key to the recipient.

The RSA process can therefore produce an authenticated message *or* a secure message, depending on whether we encrypt with a private key or a public key. Ideally we'd like messages to be both authenticated and secure. We can accomplish this by applying both variations of the process to the same message. In our example, illustrated in Figure 3-8, Abigail could encrypt the number she wants to transmit with her private key, then encrypt the result with Zed's public key. Upon receipt, Zed would reverse the procedures, first decrypting with his private key, then again with Abigail's public key.

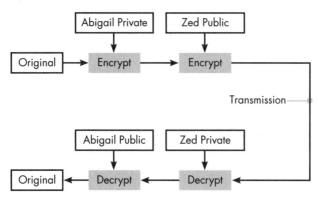

Figure 3-8: Applying the RSA with the sender's private key and the recipient's public key provides authentication and security.

Identity Authorities

You may have noticed that authentication introduces a subtler version of the shared key problem. Zed knew the email came from Abigail because he recognized the PIN produced when he transformed the number using Abigail's public key, which means the sender must have the matching private key. But if Zed is worried about someone pretending to be Abigail, how exactly does he know that the public key was sent by Abigail in the first place, not by an imposter who has hacked Abigail's email account?

The solution to this problem is an *authority*, a third party that helps verify identities. As you'll see, authorities provide the digital equivalent of ID cards. When two computers initiate a secure, authenticated transmission through the exchange of public keys, they show their IDs, which assures each computer of the identity of the other. Of course, this assumes each computer trusts the authority providing the ID, so in the end, authentication requires having implicit faith in someone. One either trusts that the transmission comes from the entity that claims to have sent it, or one trusts some third party to identify the sender. Identity authorities form a crucial component of the ultimate subject of this chapter, web security.

Security on the Web: HTTPS

Web pages are transferred using HTTP, which stands for *Hypertext Transfer Protocol*. When this data is transferred securely, it is called HTTPS, where the *S* stands for *secure*. This is why you'll see *https* at the beginning of your browser's address bar when you are transferring sensitive data—or I hope you do. Web security is something most people take for granted, but it's an amazing feat to instantly create trust and security between two automated parties who may have just been introduced, requiring all the tricks and techniques you've seen so far.

For this discussion, suppose you're purchasing from a retail website using a computer or phone. In this scenario, your computer is known as the *client*. The computer running the website for the retailer is the *server*. This is the first time you've made a purchase from this retailer, so you have to provide shipping and billing information such as your address and credit card number. This situation cries out for security, but it requires authentication as well.

To see why, you have to remember that your computer is not directly connected to the server. Your data will be passed along from system to system, through computers managed by your Internet service provider (ISP) and those managed by the retailer's ISP, and possibly through intermediate systems managed by neither. It's possible for any of these systems to be compromised by attackers such that the infected system would intercept transmissions headed for the retailer, responding in its place. If this happens, when you place your order, you're giving your data away to attackers, not to the retailer. Although the data is encrypted, it is encrypted with the key provided by the compromised system, so the encryption ensures only that no one else eavesdrops on the data you are sending to the attackers. This sort of impersonation is known as a *man-in-the-middle* attack, and is foiled by good authentication.

Handshaking

Secure transmission of data occurs in sessions. A *session* is the web equivalent of a phone call: an extended conversation that begins when you first load a page on a site and ends after you have not interacted with the site for some predetermined amount of time.

Before the transmission can begin, your client and the server must successfully perform a ritual called *handshaking*. The name implies that it's just two computers saying howdy, but it's more like a tense scene in a crime show where one guy doesn't want to show the "stuff" in the back of the van until the other guy shows the cash in the briefcase. The handshaking phase, if successful, authenticates the server to the client, and creates the key that will be used for encrypting the data throughout the session. As with Abigail and Zed, a public-key encryption system is used just long enough to share the keys needed for the better-performing private-key encryption system.

Step 1

The client tells the server which encryption methods it supports. The HTTPS protocol allows computers to choose from a suite of acceptable methods for encryption, which means that different secure websites that you access may use different encryption techniques providing higher or lower levels of security. In addition to the encryption support information, the client also provides a randomly generated number—the purpose of which you'll soon see.

Step 2

The server responds with its own list of supported encryption methods and also its *certificate*. The server certificate contains several pieces of data, including the domain name of the site (such as amazon.com) and the name of the certificate *issuer* (the authority that will verify the site's identity). It also contains the server's public key. HTTPS can use several different public-key cryptographic systems, but RSA is common. The server uses the same certificate for every client it transacts with, so the public-and-private key pair only has to be created once for each certificate. Although this means the server uses the same RSA keys for all clients, as you'll see, the RSA keys are used only during this handshaking phase.

The server certificate also contains a *signature*. As discussed in Chapter 2, digital signatures are hash codes. In this case, the server hashes the certificate data and encrypts the hash code using the server's private key.

In addition, the server also sends a random number to the client, just as the client has sent a random number to the server.

Step 3

The client validates the certificate. There are two aspects to the validation. First, the client applies the server's public key to the hash code in the certificate, then hashes the certificate itself and compares the two hash codes. If the codes match, the certificate is internally valid, but it doesn't prove this is the actual certificate for the site.

Now the client must check with the issuer of the certificate, a certification authority with built-in trust with your browser. If you drill down into your browser's options, you will find a list of issuers under a heading such as "Trusted root certification authorities." The issuer provides a copy of the site's certificate; when this matches the certificate provided by the server, the client is assured of the identity of the server.

Step 4

The client generates another random number, 48 bytes long, or 384 bits, known as the *premaster secret*. As the name implies, this number must remain a secret. However, the client needs to send it to the server, so the client encrypts it using the server's public key.

Step 5

The client and server independently create the 384-bit *master secret* by hashing a combination of the premaster secret and the two random numbers that were exchanged in the first two steps. Once the master secret is created, the premaster secret and the other two random numbers are discarded.

Note that the master secret is not exchanged between client and server. By this stage, both the client and the server have all the numbers needed to create the master secret. They independently run the numbers through the same process to produce the same result.

A summary of the handshaking process is shown in Figure 3-9.

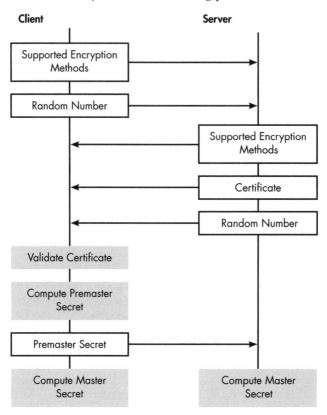

Figure 3-9: The HTTPS handshaking procedure

Transmitting Data Under HTTPS

Now the client and server can begin sending actual data—web pages and media from the server, and user data from the client. The 384 bits of the master secret are divided into three 128-bit sections, each providing a different aspect of security.

Data Encryption

The first section of the master secret is used as the key for a private-key encryption system such as AES. Each of the subsequent data transmissions during the secure session will be encrypted using this cipher key.

Block Chaining

Because web pages have standard header formats that could provide cribs to attackers, a method such as block chaining (discussed in Chapter 1) is employed. As you may recall, such systems need a starting value to encrypt the first block of the transmission; the middle 128-bit section of the master secret is used as this starting value.

Message Authentication Code

The final 128-bit section of the master secret is used to create a *message authentication code*, or *MAC*, for each transmission. In this case, we're not trying to authenticate the identity of the sender—that was already handled in the handshaking phase. Instead, the MAC ensures that data isn't altered during transmission.

In this process, each transmission is hashed through a function like MD5, but first the transmission data is combined with the remaining 128-bit section of the master secret. This is known as *keyed hashing*, and the 128-bit section in this context is known as a *MAC key*. Using a keyed hash helps foil man-in-the-middle attacks. An attacker who wishes to pass a fake transmission to the receiver will need the MAC key to produce a hash code that will be accepted as genuine by the receiver.

The hashing occurs before the encryption, so that both the original message and the hash code are encrypted.

The Shared Key Problem Solved?

So that's how data is securely transmitted over the Web. As you can see, solving the shared key problem requires just about every trick in the cryptography toolkit. Public-key encryption creates the secure channel for initial communications. Private-key encryption is used to secure individual transmissions of data. Hashing authenticates both the session and individual messages. If the site uses passwords to authenticate users, then all of the password techniques from Chapter 2 would come into play as well.

Web security is a complex system of techniques. And therein lies a potential problem: the complexity of computer security can hide weaknesses. Just as a machine with more parts has more parts that can break down, the layering of so many intricate methods and techniques can mask undiscovered vulnerabilities. Sometimes the vulnerability is not within any one part, but in how the parts are connected. Although methods like RSA and AES are currently considered safe, clever attackers may find ways to break the security without breaking the underlying encryption methods.

For example, earlier versions of HTTPS were vulnerable to a particular man-in-the-middle attack that arose from the observation that most secure sessions begin with a user clicking on a link. Suppose, for example, that you have received an email from the bank that issues your credit card with a link to your most recent account statement. The link is an HTTPS address, which means that when you click it, your browser will launch and request a secure connection with the bank's server. However, this request itself is not secure. An attacker's program could intercept this request and pass it along to the bank server as a request for a plain unencrypted HTTP connection, and then eavesdrop on all the unencrypted traffic that followed. The user might be tipped off by the prefix in the address bar, but how many users would think to check that? To cover this security hole, web servers can now tell browsers that all connections must be made through HTTPS—but that solution doesn't foil an attacker who can intercept the announcement as well. The ultimate solution may be to require HTTPS for all web communications.

Undoubtedly new vulnerabilities will be found in the future, requiring the invention of new defenses. Computer security is a moving target. We'll never be able to declare our data entirely safe, but relying on best practices may keep us one step ahead of attackers.

4

MOVIE CGI

Some of software's most impressive work can be seen in movie theaters. Images that in earlier eras were painstakingly produced with models, matte paintings, elaborate costumes, and trick photography are now created by computers. More than merely simplifying the filmmaking process, *computer-generated imagery (CGI)* produces images that would have been impossible before. For many filmgoers, movies changed forever when they saw *Jurassic Park*. When Steven Spielberg was developing the movie, he expected to create his dinosaurs using old-school effects like automated puppets and animated miniatures, but once he saw some computer-animated test footage, he decided to use CGI for many of the dinosaur shots. The result left viewers astounded by images like the panorama shown in Figure 4-1. For comparison, the old way to put a dinosaur in a movie is shown in Figure 4-2.

Figure 4-1: CGI dinosaurs visit the watering hole in Jurassic Park *(Universal Pictures/ Amblin Entertainment, 1993).*

Figure 4-2: The Beast from 20,000 Fathoms (Jack Dietz Productions, 1953) munches on Coney Island.

Amazing as they were, films like *Jurassic Park* were just the beginning of the CGI revolution. Now movies like *Avatar* create whole worlds using CGI, so that viewers are never sure what parts of a shot are physically real, if any. With enough time and money, it seems like filmmakers can produce anything imaginable.

Before computers blew our minds with dinosaurs and lush alien planets, though, they were transforming the world of traditionally animated movies. Using computers not only radically altered the process of traditional animation, but as you'll discover, the concepts and techniques employed are the foundation for almost everything in computer graphics. This is where the story of CGI begins.

Software for Traditional Animation

A movie is a series of still images, or *frames*, presented to the eye in rapid succession, like a high-speed slideshow. Each frame lingers on the retina for a moment after it disappears from the screen, effectively blending with the next frame to provide the illusion of continuous motion—a phenomenon known as *persistence of vision*. Traditionally, movies are shown at a rate of 24 frames per second (fps). Making a movie means producing 24 images for every second of the film.

A live-action movie uses a camera to collect images in real time. A traditionally animated film like *Lady and the Tramp*, though, is created a bit differently: each frame of the movie is an individually photographed, handcrafted work of art.

Traditional animation is a huge undertaking requiring a large team of artists. Typically, each character in an animated film is assigned a lead animator, but the lead animator does not draw the character on every frame in which he or she appears, because that's too much work for one person. Instead, the lead animator draws only as many *keyframes* as are needed to suggest the action—perhaps one out of every few dozen frames of a finished animation sequence. Other animators draw the in-between frames to complete the sequence, a process known as *tweening*. At this stage, the animation is still just a series of pencil drawings on paper. The drawings must be transferred to transparent cellulose sheets, which is why this style of animation is also known as *cel animation*. Then comes what animators call "ink and paint": the faint pencil lines are traced over with black ink, and the cel is colored. Then the sheets are placed in front of a separately painted background and photographed.

As you might expect, tweening, inking, and painting are tedious, time-intensive jobs. Beginning around 1990, computer imagery has been used to mimic the cel animation style with far less manual labor.

How Digital Images Work

In a traditional animated film, each frame is a photograph of physical art, but computer animation works with *digital images*—pictures defined by numerical data.

When you look at a video display such as a television, a smartphone screen, or a digitally projected theater screen, the image that reaches your eyes is made up of dots of varying colors, known as *pixels*. Figure 4-3 depicts a tree against a blue sky as a grid of pixels. Each of the 100 pixels in this 10×10 grid is assigned a color, here specified by name.

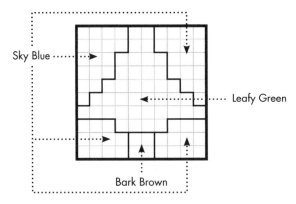

Sky Blue

Leafy Green

Bark Brown

Figure 4-3: A tree made of pixels

Although we can think of each pixel as a solid color, the underlying reality is a bit different. For example, at home you might watch a movie on a common *liquid crystal display (LCD)* television in which pixel colors are determined by electrically controlled crystals. On the back of an LCD screen is a light source, either a fluorescent lamp or a series of *light-emitting diodes (LEDs)*. The light source itself is white. In front of the light is a translucent panel with bars in the three primary colors—red, green, and blue—as shown in Figure 4-4.

A layer of liquid crystals lying between the light source and the color panel puts an individually controlled crystal behind each of the translucent bars.

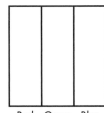

Red   Green   Blue

Figure 4-4: Three bars of pure primary colors create one LCD pixel.

You can think of these crystals as electrically operated doors, and the degree to which each crystal door is open determines how much light gets through. By varying the amount of red, green, or blue, any one of millions of colors can be produced by each pixel. This is *additive color mixing*, in which adding more color makes the result brighter. If we want a particular pixel to come across as bright yellow, for example, we would set the levels of red and green high, and the level of blue low. If we wanted a dark gray, we would set each of the color bars to the same low intensity. All three colors at maximum intensity produce pure white. Later in this chapter, we'll see an example of *subtractive color mixing*, which is what you might remember from art class, where adding more color makes the result darker.

How Colors Are Defined

The most common way to define a pixel's color is with the *RGB* system, which uses three numbers to represent the intensity of red, green, and blue in the pixel. The numbers typically range from 0 to 255 to match the range of an eight-bit byte. This means that each RGB pixel is specified by three bytes of data.

As far as software is concerned, a digital image such as that shown in Figure 4-3 is just a list of bytes of color data, three bytes for each pixel. This block of bytes is known as the image's *bitmap*. The first three bytes in the bitmap are the red, green, and blue levels of the pixel in the upper-left corner of the image, and so on. The width and height of an image or bitmap in pixels is known as its *resolution*; for instance, Figure 4-3's resolution is 10×10. A bitmap called a *display buffer* stores the colors of each pixel of a digital display like an LCD television; ultimately, computer graphics methods are about setting the numbers in a display buffer.

The location of a particular pixel in a bitmap is specified by two *coordinates*, an *x*-coordinate for horizontal position and a *y*-coordinate for vertical position. The (0,0) coordinate, known as the *origin*, can be located in a corner or in the center; it varies among different coordinate systems. When positioning pixels on a physical display, we refer to coordinates as *screen coordinates*. Screen coordinate systems commonly set the origin at the upper-left pixel, so a 1920×1080 screen would locate pixels as shown in Figure 4-5. Here, the y-axis increases moving down the image, the x-axis increases moving right across the image, and the center location is (960, 540).

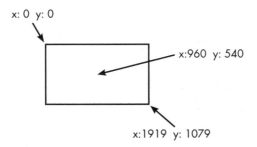

Figure 4-5: Locating pixels on a 1920x1080 screen

Coordinate systems are a ubiquitous part of computer graphics and, as you'll see in this chapter and the next, much of the work of producing graphics involves converting coordinates from one system to another.

How Software Makes Cel Animations

Now that you understand what's inside a digital image, you're ready to see how software can make digital images that look like traditional cels. The first step is getting the artist's work inside the computer.

Transforming Drawings into Models

Software-generated cel animation starts the same way as traditional animation: with an artist sketching a character. Instead of drawing on paper, though, the artist draws with a mouse or an electronic stylus and the drawings are recorded by software. In order to ultimately produce a bitmapped image, we need a system that defines the artist's strokes numerically, producing a *model* of the drawing. Locations within a model are called *local coordinates*. Figure 4-6 shows a drawing of a bug-man within a box that defines the local coordinate space.

x: 0 y: 0

x:1000 y: 1000

Figure 4-6: A bug-man drawing inside a box defining coordinate limits

Each line and curve in this model is defined in terms of these local coordinates. Straight line segments, like the antennae and legs of our character, can be defined by the coordinates of the points at either end of the line, as shown in Figure 4-7. Note that the coordinates here have fractional parts to increase precision.

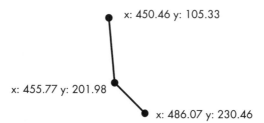

x: 450.46 y: 105.33

x: 455.77 y: 201.98

x: 486.07 y: 230.46

Figure 4-7: Defining straight line segments using the coordinates of the end points

For curves, *control points* are needed in addition to end points to define the direction and amount of curvature. Imagine that the control point is attached to the curve so that moving it controls the degree of curvature, as illustrated by the simple curves in Figure 4-8. If you've ever worked with a vector graphics application, you've likely worked with curves like this.

Figure 4-8: Curves defined by two end points and one control point

Simple curves can be represented by just two end points and one control point, but longer, more complicated curves are made up of sequences of simple curves, as shown with the bug-man's shoe in Figure 4-9.

Figure 4-9: A complicated curve made of simple curves

The lines and curves define just the outline of a character or other drawing; the colors inside the outline are defined using a system such as RGB. The character model, then, is a numerical representation of all the lines, curves, and color data.

Automatic Tweening

Numerically defining drawings allows for automatic tweening. The animator draws one frame of a character's animation sequence, then creates succeeding keyframes by moving the control points of the curves in the previous frames. The animation software can then generate the other frames through *interpolation*. The concept is demonstrated in Figure 4-10. Here, the coordinates of the middle point are calculated as the average of the coordinates of the other points. The x-coordinate of the interpolated point, 20, is halfway between 10 and 30; the y-coordinate, 120, is halfway between 100 and 140. In this example, all the points lie on a line, but the interpolation path can be a curve as well.

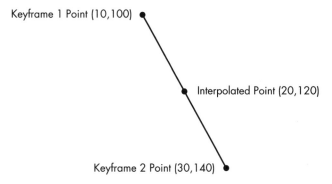

Figure 4-10: Computing a middle point between two keyframe points via interpolation

Figure 4-11 shows how interpolation creates new frames of animation. The leftmost face is the original model; the second face shows some of the control points; and the third has a wide mouth created by repositioning two of the control points downward. The rightmost face was created through linear interpolation, placing each control point halfway between the two keyframe positions. Animation software can create as many in-between positions as necessary to fill the gap between keyframes.

Figure 4-11: From left: a model, the model with selected control points, the model with two of the control points moved, and a tweened model created by interpolation between the positions of the previous two models

Although basic interpolation tweening can be a huge time-saver, adjusting the positions of lots of little points remains tedious. More advanced animation software can treat a character drawing as a complete, interconnected body, in which rigid connections and joints are specified. This means that an animator need only position the feet for each keyframe to make our bug-man walk, and the software positions the rest of the legs accordingly. The software might even handle real-world physics, so that a sequence of images of our bug-man falling over a log could be animated entirely by the software.

Positioning and Scaling

Numerical modeling also allows the drawings to be placed anywhere in a frame at any size. Changing the size of a model is called *scaling*, and is accomplished by multiplying or dividing the coordinates for each of the points. Figure 4-12 shows the bug-man model of Figure 4-6 scaled down to a quarter of its original area by dividing each of the coordinates in half. One point on his antenna is highlighted to show the idea.

Placing a model in a particular location on the screen is called *translation*, and is accomplished by increasing or decreasing coordinates by fixed amounts. In Figure 4-13, the shrunken bug-man from Figure 4-12 is translated to the middle of the screen by adding 700 to each x-coordinate and 200 to each y-coordinate.

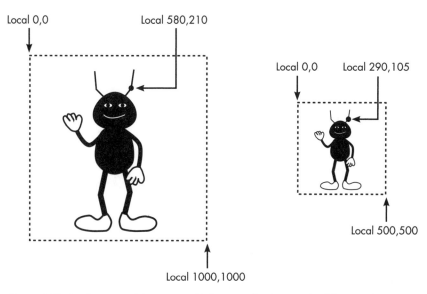

Figure 4-12: Scaling a model means multiplying or dividing each of the coordinates.

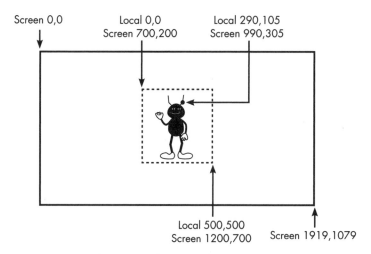

Figure 4-13: Translating a model means adding to or subtracting from coordinates.

"Ink and Paint" for Digital Images

Now that the points on the models are mapped to screen coordinates, it's time to transform each frame into a bitmap. This is the software version of cel animation's "ink and paint." To keep things simple, let's look at how just the right arm of our bug-man model would be converted to a bitmap, or *rasterized*, when displayed over a solid white background. Figure 4-14 shows the arm over a pixel grid, with circles marking the pixel centers.

With the model mathematically defined, the software can place the arm at any position on the bitmap and then apply the indicated color—in this case, black—to the appropriate pixels. Right away we see there's a problem, though: the contours of the arm don't match the borders of pixels, so how do we determine which pixels to color? A simple rule is to color pixels when their centers are covered. Figure 4-15 shows the result of pixel-center coloring.

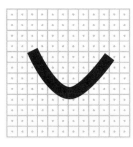

Figure 4-14: The right arm of the bug-man super-imposed over a pixel grid

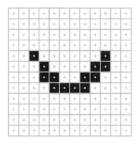

Figure 4-15: Coloring pixels solid black based on pixel centers

As you can see, though, this result is rather ugly. Because the pixels are square, this coloring rule replaces the gracefully curving border of the model with a jagged edge, which is why this problem is known as *the jaggies*. The general problem is that the model is smooth and continuous, while the bitmap is made with square black-and-white pixels. The bitmap is just an approximation of the model. The discrepancy between continuous models and their bitmap approximations is known as *aliasing*, and is the source of many visual anomalies in computer graphics.

To avoid the jaggies, we need to color pixels using an *anti-aliasing* technique. In our example, instead of coloring the pixels black and white, we'll use a range of grays to produce a better approximation of the model. Each pixel will be colored based on how much of it is covered by the arm.

In order to put this idea into action, instead of checking only the center of each pixel, let's test several points in each pixel to see how many of them lie within the model. In Figure 4-16, 7 of the 10 testing points scattered around the pixel area are covered by the shape, meaning this is 70 percent coverage.

The percentage of each pixel covered by the model determines the gray level. The result for our bug-man's arm is shown in Figure 4-17. Although this example might not look like much, if you hold the page at arm's length and squint, the edges should appear to smoothly blend into the white background, producing the illusion of a graceful curve.

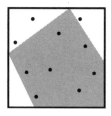

Figure 4-16: A close-up of one pixel at the end of the bug-man's arm, with a scattering of 10 points to estimate the area covered by the model

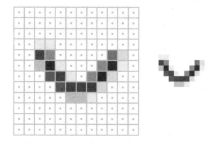

Figure 4-17: Using grayscale to anti-alias, shown with and without the pixel grid.

Blending into Any Background

We need to generalize the technique just described in order for it to work with a background other than solid white. Consider Figure 4-18. On the left is the bug-man model, and in the middle is the background for the shot in which he'll appear: a close-up of a setting sun over a rocky terrain. On the right is the complete image with the model superimposed over the background.

Model   Background   Model over Background

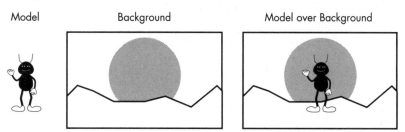

Figure 4-18: The bug-man model, a background, and the model superimposed over the background

This book is printed in black and white, but in this image the sun would be shades of reddish-orange and the ground would be shades of brown. As before, pixels along the model's edge will appear jagged unless we use an anti-aliasing technique. But using the previous technique to color pixels in gray tones won't help the black edge blend into a background of red-orange and brown pixels.

A more general anti-aliasing technique calculates an *alpha level* for each pixel based on the percentage of the pixel that's covered by the model. You can think of an alpha level as a measure of opacity. Like the color levels, an alpha level is typically defined in the range of 0–255. In Figure 4-19, a black bar is superimposed over a tree at different alpha levels. At an alpha level of 255, the bar is entirely opaque, while at 25 the bar is barely visible. An alpha level of 0 would make the bar completely invisible.

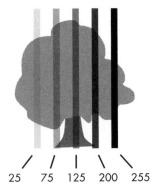

The alpha levels of all the pixels in a bitmap are collectively referred to as its *alpha channel*. The process of making an alpha channel for a model is similar to how we anti-aliased the black arm against the white background, only rather than assigning a shade of gray based on the pixel's coverage percentage, we assign an alpha value for the pixel instead. Each model is thus conceptually transformed into both a bitmap, showing the color of each pixel covered by the model, and an alpha channel, showing the opacity of each pixel. Figure 4-20 shows the color bitmap (here, just black pixels) and the alpha channel of the bug-man arm separately.

Figure 4-19: A tree covered by five black bars of varying alpha level

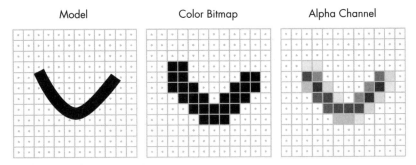

Figure 4-20: The arm of the bug-man model with its corresponding color bitmap and alpha channel

Now the model can be applied to any background. The final color of each pixel is a blend of the color in the background and the model's color bitmap, with the alpha level determining how much of each color goes into the mix. In the bug-man scene of Figure 4-18, if a black bug-man pixel with 30 percent alpha were placed on top of a red-orange sunset background pixel, the result would be a darker red-orange, as shown in Figure 4-21. The resulting amount of each color component lies somewhere between the two mixed colors, but because the black pixel is only 30 percent alpha, the red-orange background color dominates. For pixels completely covered by the model, the alpha level is 100 percent and the color in the final image is the same as in the model's color bitmap. In this way, a bitmap with an alpha channel can be smoothly blended into any background.

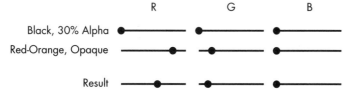

Figure 4-21: The red, green, and blue components of three colors: the black of the model, the red-orange of the background pixel, and the result of mixing these two colors if the black has 30% alpha

From Cel Animation Software to Rendered 2D Graphics

These techniques are now the default way to produce cel-style animation, and software is as common a tool for animation studios as brushes and paper were in earlier generations. While some animation studios use programs they developed themselves, most direct-to-video or television animation and some feature films are made with off-the-shelf software. One such program, Toon Boom, has been used for television shows such as *The Simpsons* and *Phineas and Ferb*, while the artists at Studio Ghibli use a program called Toonz to animate such movies as *Spirited Away*.

The usefulness of these techniques is not limited to filmmaking, though. More generally, the software techniques used to mimic traditional cel-style animation are called two-dimensional graphics, or *2D graphics*, because the control points for models are located with two coordinates, x and y. The general task of transforming models into final images is called *rendering*, and the software that performs the task is the *renderer*. Rendered 2D graphics are used throughout computing. Many video games, such as *Angry Birds*, use the cel-animation look. These rendering techniques are also used to display fonts and icons in applications such as browsers and word processors.

Although rendered 2D graphics are ubiquitous in computing and can make great cel-style animations, creating the mind-blowing visuals of films like *Avatar* requires extending these ideas to three dimensions.

Software for 3D CGI

Breathtaking CGI in films like *Avatar* use *3D graphics*. The "3D" here doesn't refer to simulated depth perception, like in a 3D movie, but rather to the three coordinates of each control point in the animation models: x- and y-coordinates for horizontal and vertical positioning and a z-coordinate to indicate depth. Figure 4-22 shows a three-dimensional model of a box with a highlighted point defined by x-, y-, and z-coordinates.

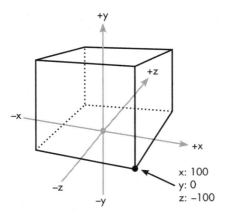

Figure 4-22: A box in three-dimensional space

As with 2D graphics, 3D graphics are all about rendering models into bitmaps. The rendering methods that produce the most realistic results require the most processing time. Movie CGI is impressive largely because the renderer can process each frame for a very long time, resulting in the high-quality result that I'll call *movie-quality rendering*. We'll discuss the keys to movie-quality rendering in this chapter. Then, in Chapter 5, we'll talk about graphics for video games, and see how many of the techniques shown here have to be modified, faked, or scrapped altogether when images must be produced in real time in response to user interaction.

How 3D Scenes Are Described

3D models are built out of lines and curves just like 2D models, but these lines and curves stretch across three dimensions instead of two. The box in Figure 4-22 is a very simple model defined by eight points; the models used in movie CGI tend to be complex, defined by hundreds, thousands, or even tens of thousands of points. As with 2D rendering, models in 3D rendering are defined by local coordinates. The points at the corners of the box in Figure 4-22, for example, are defined relative to the local origin at the bottom of the box.

While 2D rendering can directly map from local coordinates to screen coordinates, 3D models are first placed into scenes in a virtual world that has its own coordinate space called *world coordinates*. Designing a 3D scene is the CGI equivalent of building a movie set. We can place as many models as we want in the virtual world, of any size and at any location, and the renderer can figure out the world coordinates for all the locations on the models.

Introducing another coordinate system might seem like an unnecessary complication, but world coordinates actually make 3D graphics much easier in the long run. For example, an artist can model a dining room chair independently of the other models for the scene in which it will be used. Then the artist can copy the single chair model to make as many seats as needed for the dining room scene. Also, a scene, like a movie set, isn't built to produce a single image but to create a space that will be shown in many images from many different angles, as we'll see in the next section.

The Virtual Camera

With the scenery in place, a *viewpoint* is needed. On a movie set, a cinematographer determines what image is captured by placing the camera and choosing a lens. For CGI, the viewpoint determines how the three-dimensional scene is transformed into a two-dimensional rendered image.

Transformation from three dimensions to two is known as *projection*. To better understand projection, consider Figure 4-23, in which an imaginary pyramid originates from the eye of a viewer looking at a table. A translucent grid lies in the pyramid between the viewer and the scene. Looking through the grid, the viewer can map each visible location on the three-dimensional table to a particular square on the two-dimensional grid. That's projection, but instead of a grid of squares, it's a grid of pixels in a bitmap.

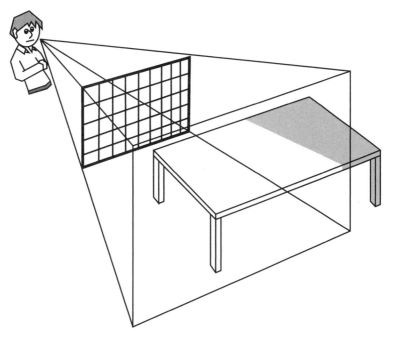

Figure 4-23: Projecting a three-dimensional scene onto a flat display is like viewing a real-world scene through a translucent grid.

Direct Lighting

There are many different methods of projection, but projection methods in movie-quality rendering are part of the larger issue of lighting. Although we don't often realize it, our perception of an object's color is determined not only by the object itself but also by the lighting under which we view the object. Knowing this, filmmakers carefully light their scenes for dramatic effect, but the problem of lighting in CGI is more fundamental. Without an accurate model of scene lighting, the resulting images won't look realistic at all.

To understand why this is true, let's take a simple scene of a yellow metal table in a green room, as shown in Figure 4-24.

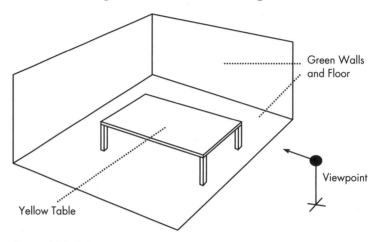

Figure 4-24: A 3D scene

From this viewpoint, some of the pixels will be "table" pixels and the others will be "wall" or "floor" pixels. A simple renderer might color every table pixel the same shade of yellow, while coloring all the other pixels an identical green. But because this coloring ignores the effect of lighting, the resulting image would be flat and unrealistic. (The blocks of solid color would make the image resemble an animation cel—an interesting effect, but not realistic.) A movie-quality renderer needs a *lighting model* so that the colors in our scenes are influenced by virtual light sources.

The essential real-world lighting effects modeled by CGI renderers include distance, diffuse reflection, and specular reflection.

The Distance Effect

To understand the distance effect, imagine a lamp emitting pure white light hanging directly over the middle of the table, as in Figure 4-25.

The closer this light is to the table, the brighter the table appears. In the physical world, this effect is caused by the beam of light widening as it gets farther from its source. The more narrowly focused a light source is, the less the light diminishes with distance—which explains why the highly focused light of a laser hardly diminishes at all.

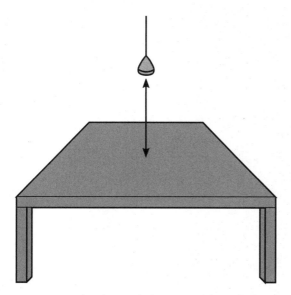

Figure 4-25: The closer a light is to a surface, the brighter the surface appears.

Renderers can model the distance effect realistically, but they also allow unrealistic distance effects in order to create a particular look or mood. For example, in a scene where a character carries a torch through a cave, a lighting designer will decide whether the torchlight extends a long way or barely penetrates the gloom.

All of the lighting effects we'll discuss allow these kinds of adjustments. Although it may seem strange to intentionally create unrealistic light when the whole point of the lighting model is to make a realistic scene, there's a subtle but important distinction between reality and viewers' expectations of reality. Using light in unrealistic ways is an old cinematic trick. For example, when a character in a darkened bedroom turns on a lamp, a stage light in the ceiling of the set also turns on, so that the entire scene is softly lit. Without the extra, unrealistic light, the scene won't look right—it will appear too dark. In the same way, CGI lighting models allow their controls to be tweaked to produce results that are a little wrong, but feel right.

The Diffuse Reflection Effect

Light that strikes a surface head-on appears brighter than light that strikes a surface at a sharp angle. In Figure 4-26, the center of the table seems brighter, or yellower, than the corners.

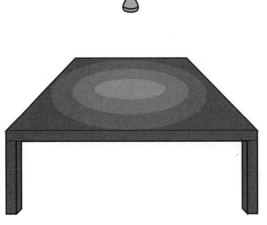

Figure 4-26: Diffuse lighting depends on the angle at which light strikes a surface.

This is due in part to the distance effect—the center is closer to the lamp than the corners—but is mostly due to the *diffuse reflection* effect, a change in brightness caused by variation in the light's *angle of incidence*. In Figure 4-27, the solid lines show the incident light rays, while the dashed lines are reflections. As you can see, the light strikes point B at a much larger angle than at point A, and therefore point B appears brighter than point A. But note that the *viewing angle*, or *angle of reflectance*, makes no difference in the diffuse reflection effect. Therefore, point A will look the same to both viewers, and so will point B.

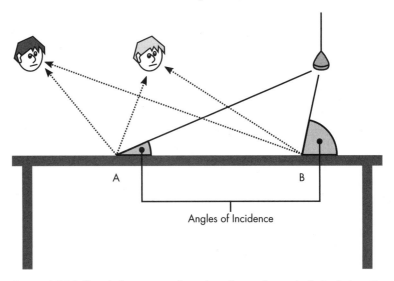

Figure 4-27: Diffuse lighting varies based on the angle at which the light strikes the surface, but is the same for all viewpoints.

The Specular Reflection Effect

Because the metal tabletop is highly reflective, it partially acts as a mirror. As with any mirror, what you see in it depends on what lies on the opposite angle to your point of view. Figure 4-28 shows a shiny spot on the table where the hanging light is at the opposite angle from our viewpoint, approximately midway between the center of the table and the closest edge. Because this spot is a mirror-like reflection of the white light bulb, the spot will be white.

Figure 4-28: Specular lighting depends on both the angle at which the light strikes the surface and the view angle.

These shiny spots are known as *specular reflections*, and appear where the light's angle of incidence matches the angle of reflectance. Figure 4-29 shows the location of specular reflections for two different viewpoints; notice that each ray rebounds at the same angle that it struck the table. Both viewers see a shiny spot on the table, but they see the spot in different places.

In the real world, some materials reflect differently than others. A shiny material like plastic has a high level of specular reflection, while a dull material like cotton cloth has more diffuse reflection. CGI lighting models allow artists to set different reflection properties for each surface on a model to match the appearance of real-world materials.

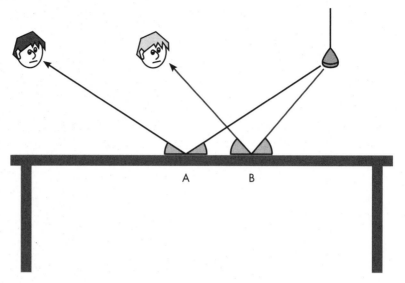

Figure 4-29: The specular light on the table appears in different places for different viewpoints.

Global Illumination

So far we've been discussing *direct lighting*, the result of light flowing directly from a source to a surface. In reality, the color of every object in the physical world is influenced by the color of every other object nearby. A light-brown sofa in a room with white walls looks very different than it does in a room with blue walls, because the sofa gains a subtle tint from the reflected light of the walls. This is *indirect lighting*, and for a computer-generated image to look realistic, it must account for this effect. A lighting model that accounts for all of the light in the scene, both direct and indirect, is known as a *global illumination model*.

An example of indirect lighting is shown in Figure 4-30. Let's assume the light bulb emits pure white light. The beam first hits a wall that is painted cyan (a light blue). The light reflecting from the wall is likewise cyan, and when the reflected cyan light strikes the yellow rug, the resulting reflected light is green. The bouncing colors therefore result in a subtle greenish tint in the yellow rug. This sequence of color changes is caused by *subtractive color*, where mixing colors results in a darker shade, the way a color inkjet makes different shades by mixing cyan, yellow, and magenta ink. Subtractive color is the opposite of the additive RGB system we discussed early in the chapter, in which mixing results in a brighter color.

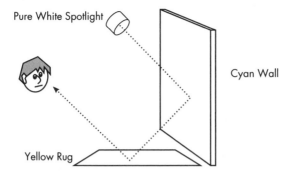

Pure White Spotlight

Cyan Wall

Yellow Rug

Figure 4-30: Light bouncing off multiple surfaces influences apparent color.

How Light Is Traced

A global illumination model seems to require following the paths of light beams as they bounce around the scene. A naive renderer, then, would use three-dimensional coordinate math to trace the path of every beam of light from each light source as it bounces from surface to surface. This would waste a lot effort, though, because it would deduce the color of every surface in the scene—including surfaces the viewer can't actually see because they lie outside of the viewpoint's field of view, are obscured by other objects, or are facing away from the viewpoint.

Why Light Is Traced Backward

Renderers avoid this inefficiency by tracing beams backward from the viewpoint into the scene, a technique known as *ray tracing*. In ray tracing, an imaginary line is traced from the viewpoint through the center of each square in a pixel grid, as shown in Figure 4-31. The geometry of each model in the scene is compared with the imaginary line to see if the two intersect. The closest point of intersection to the viewpoint indicates the visible surface that will color the pixel. Note that this method of projection closely follows the explanation of Figure 4-23.

Next, more lines are traced outward from this known visible point. The goal is to discover which lines end at light sources, either directly or after bouncing off other objects. As shown in Figure 4-31, specular reflections trace only the rebound at the same angle of each impact, but diffuse reflections trace a number of lines in random directions. As the diffuse beams strike other objects, they will spawn more diffuse reflections, which means the number of paths to trace keeps multiplying the more the process continues. Renderers apply a cut-off to limit the number of bounces for each beam.

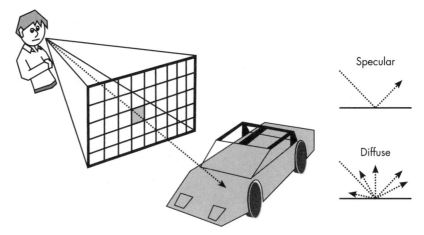

Figure 4-31: Tracing a beam of light from a viewpoint, through the center of the shaded pixel, until it reaches a model in the scene. To determine specular lighting, the tracing rebounds at the same angle as impact; for diffuse lighting, it rebounds at several random angles.

How Ray Tracing Models Real-World Effects

Although ray tracing is a lot of work for even a network of computers, the method can accurately model many real-world visual effects.

One such effect is translucency. Although a bitmap can be made translucent by assigning low alpha values to pixels, that's not the whole story for transparent materials like glass. A glass tumbler, for example, doesn't merely allow light to pass through it, but also distorts whatever is behind it, as shown in Figure 4-32.

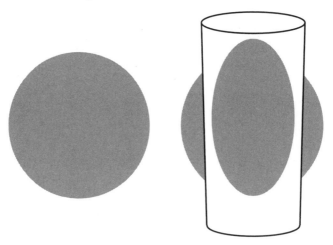

Figure 4-32: The distortion of curved glass

A ray tracing renderer can refract light beams according to the laws of optics as they pass through translucent materials. This will not only allow the renderer to model glass in CGI, but will also help to reproduce the distorting effects of transparent materials and liquids like water.

Ray tracing can also be extended to simulate camera lenses. Normally, all objects in a computer-generated image are perfectly in focus. In images shot by a movie camera, though, only objects at a certain distance from the camera are in focus, leaving other objects less focused the farther they are from that distance. While one might consider having everything in focus an *advantage* of computer-generated imagery, skilled cinematographers use selective focus to help tell their stories. In Figure 4-33, Jimmy Stewart and Grace Kelly are in focus in the foreground, while the apartments in the background are blurry; the viewer's attention is drawn to the actors, but the distant, open background is a subtle reminder of how visible the apartments in this courtyard are from each other—an important detail in the film. Because movie viewers have grown accustomed to receiving depth information about scenes through the use of focus, computer-generated images and movies often must simulate the use of photography lenses to match viewer expectations.

Figure 4-33: Focus depth in Rear Window *(Paramount Pictures/Patron Inc., 1954)*

Shadows are another key component of a realistic computer-generated image. Ray tracing produces shadows naturally, as shown in Figure 4-34. Because no beam of light can reach the shadowed area, no beam traced back from the viewpoint can reach the light, so the area will remain dark.

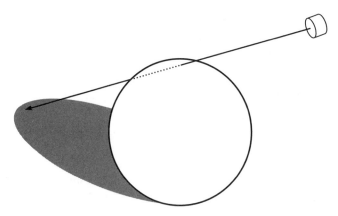

Figure 4-34: Tracing beams of light renders shadows naturally.

Ray tracing can also model highly reflective surfaces simply by setting a very high specular reflection property on the material. For example, when you're standing inside a well-lit room when it's dark outside, the room in which you stand is clearly reflected in the window.

So although ray tracing is computationally intense, adding these real-world effects doesn't add much extra work, and the effects add greatly to the realism of the final image. In the next chapter, you'll see the tricks video games use to render reflective surfaces and shadowing in real time, when ray tracing isn't an option. Some effects, like glass distortion, are usually not even attempted in real-time rendering; there's simply not enough time.

Full-Scene Anti-Aliasing

While the images rendered by ray tracing can be stunning, they can suffer from the same aliasing problems we saw with 2D graphics. Whenever one object is in front of another, each projected light beam will either hit the foreground object or miss and hit what lies behind the object. Figure 4-35 shows a chair on a rug as seen from a particular viewpoint. Beams traced from this viewpoint near the edge of the chair seat hit either the chair or the rug, which assigns the associated pixel the color of one surface or the other. This causes a jagged edge like those we saw for 2D images.

The renderer can avoid the jaggies by applying anti-aliasing to the whole image. There are many methods for *full-screen anti-aliasing*, but with ray tracing, a direct way to anti-alias the entire scene is to project more beams from the viewpoint than necessary. For example, rather than just sending out a beam at the center of every pixel, the renderer might also send out beams into the spaces between the pixel centers. After the color for every beam is determined, the final color of each pixel is blended from the colors of the center beam and the beams at the neighboring corners. Pixels that lie along an edge in the image are thereby assigned intermediate colors, avoiding the jagged "staircase" effect.

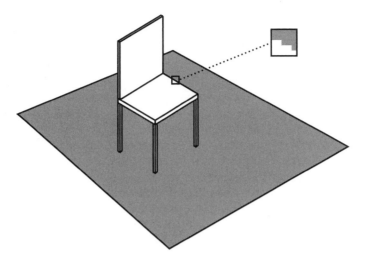

Figure 4-35: In the highlighted area, each light beam trace ends on the chair or the rug, resulting in jaggies.

Figure 4-36 demonstrates this idea. Each circle represents a beam projected into a scene. The pixels are colored based on the average of colors in the center and corners of each pixel, which results in the anti-aliased edge shown on the right. More beams can be traced for even better results, at the expense of more processing time.

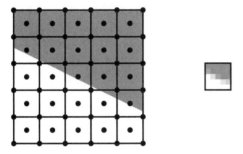

Figure 4-36: Each pixel's final color is a blend of five beams traced into the scene, one at the center of the pixel, and four at the corners.

Combining the Real and the Fake

In a completely computer-animated film, rendering is the final step in producing each frame, but when CGI is integrated into live-action films, there's more work to be done. Imagine, for example, a scene in which a computer-generated *Tyrannosaurus rex* stalks through a real field of grass.

To make this happen, we first need two sequences of digital images. One sequence shows the grass field, and has either been shot on a digital camera or on a traditional film camera and then subsequently scanned. Either way, the movements of the camera are computer controlled, which allows the camera movement to match up precisely with the movement of the virtual camera in the other sequence, the computer-generated animation of the dinosaur.

Next, the two sequences are combined, frame-by-frame, in a process called *digital composition*. Although the dinosaur sequence was produced from 3D models, at this point both sequences are simply two-dimensional bitmaps and are combined using the same method used to place our bug-man on top of the sunset back in Figure 4-18. Through the use of alpha blending, the edges of the dinosaur in each frame are smoothly blended with the field-of-grass background. Without this blending, the dinosaur will have a shimmering edge like that of a weatherman standing in front of the five-day forecast.

Digital composition is used throughout modern moviemaking, even when no computer-generated imagery is involved, such as for *dissolves* (a transition where one scene smoothly fades into the next). Formerly, dissolves were produced by a device known as an *optical printer*, which pointed a camera at a screen onto which several projectors were aimed. The camera would make a new film that combined the images of the projected films. A dissolve was accomplished by turning down the light in one projector while turning up the light on another. The results were acceptable, but you could always spot an optical printer sequence in a movie because the second-generation images would be blurry compared to the rest of the film. Now, dissolves, superimposed titles, and all sorts of other movie effects that you might not really think of as "effects" are performed with digital composition.

The Ideal of Movie-Quality Rendering

When all the advanced rendering techniques described in this chapter come together, the results can be stunningly realistic, highly stylized, or anything in between. The only real limitation on CGI is time, but that's a big limitation. The truth is, what I've been calling movie-quality rendering can be an unattainable ideal even for Hollywood. Although films can be in production for several years, there's only so much time that can be allotted for each frame. Consider the computer-animated Pixar film *WALL-E*. With a running time of 98 minutes, the film required the rendering of over 140,000 high-resolution computer images. If Pixar wanted to produce all of the images for *WALL-E* in two years, it would have to render images, on average, every eight minutes.

Even on a networked "render farm," eight minutes is not sufficient to use ray tracing, global illumination, glass refraction, and all the other high-end techniques for every single image. Faced with these practical constraints, filmmakers pick and choose which techniques to use on each sequence to maximize visual impact. When ideal rendering is required, the time is spent, but when the best effects won't be missed or the budget won't allow it, they aren't used. The renderer used at Pixar—a program called RenderMan that was originally developed at Lucasfilm—can forgo ray tracing and its massive associated computational effort, but that means many of the realism-enhancing effects have to be produced some other way.

But how is that done? What kinds of tricks are needed to render images without ray tracing—images that may not be perfectly realistic but are still amazing? To answer this question, we'll turn from Hollywood to the world of video games, where rendering is under an extreme time limitation. How extreme? If eight minutes isn't enough time to produce an ideal render, imagine trying to render an image in under 20 *milliseconds*. In the next chapter, we'll see how video games produce great graphics in a hurry.

5

GAME GRAPHICS

A modern video game is like a modern movie—a big production that requires expertise in many different technical areas. Teams of programmers develop code for audio, artificial intelligence, network connectivity, and so on. Still, the first thing you notice about a video game is the graphics.

Early video game systems like the Atari 2600 and Sega Genesis relied on premade bitmap graphics; that is, there was no rendering, not even the 2D rendering described in the previous chapter. Instead, if a video game needed to show the game's hero walking, an artist would draw several bitmaps to be shown in a repeating sequence. Backgrounds, too, were hand-drawn. Displays were low resolution and offered only a few choices for pixel colors.

As the quality of displays improved, game developers turned to other techniques to produce their bitmaps. Fighting games like *Mortal Kombat* would scan photographs of stunt actors in costume or at least use them for reference. Some games in this era would actually use rendered graphics, but not real-time rendering; instead they would prerender the bitmaps on more powerful systems over a longer period of time. The 3D game as we know it today was unknown outside of a few early experiments.

That started to change in the mid-1990s. Game consoles like the Sony PlayStation were built around 3D graphics capabilities instead of bitmaps. PC gamers began to purchase what were then called *graphics accelerators*—plug-in hardware to assist in the creation of 3D graphics. Those early 3D games were crude, both graphically and otherwise, compared to games today. Also, few 3D games were made for the PC because Microsoft had yet to build DirectX, a standardized interface between game software and graphics hardware, which meant that games had to include different code to match each manufacturer's graphics accelerator.

Even so, gamers were hooked on the new 3D gaming, and each succeeding generation of graphics hardware blew away the capabilities of the previous one. Nowhere was this generational leap more apparent than in *cut scenes*—short, prerendered videos shown at the beginning of the game to set the scene, or at critical points during the game to advance the plot. Because these videos were prerendered on expensive hardware, just like the movie CGI we discussed in Chapter 4, early cut scenes were much more impressive than the graphics during actual gameplay. As the hardware advanced, though, gameplay visuals began to match or even exceed the cut scenes of earlier games.

These days, few games use prerendered cut scenes. Although the game may still include noninteractive "movie" sequences to set up or advance the plot, they're much more likely to be rendered in real time, just like the rest of the game. That's because the real-time rendering looks so good, it's not worth it for game developers to do anything else.

And that, I think, is why I find video game graphics so amazing. They look as good as or better than the prerendered graphics I saw in earlier video games, or even in early CGI movies, and they're being produced in real time. Those two words—*real time*—look innocent enough, but they encapsulate an enormous challenge for a game renderer. To put it into numbers: if your typical gamer wants a refresh rate of 60 frames per second, each image must be rendered in a mere 1/60 of a second.

Hardware for Real-Time Graphics

The increasing quality of real-time graphics is tied to advancements in graphics hardware. Today's graphics hardware is powerful and optimized for the tasks involved in 3D graphical rendering. Although this book is about software, a brief discussion of hardware is necessary to understand why game graphics work the way they do.

The main processor inside a computer or video game console is the *central processing unit (CPU)*. These processors might have multiple *cores*, or independent processing subunits. Think of a core as an office worker. The cores inside a CPU are like fast, widely trained workers. They are good at doing just about any task, and doing it very quickly. However, they are so expensive that you can afford to have only a few of them, usually eight or fewer in a typical desktop processor, although this number will continue to rise.

By contrast, a *graphics processing unit (GPU)* will have hundreds or even thousands of cores. These cores are much simpler, and individually slower, than the cores in a CPU. Think of them as workers who can do only a few tasks well, and don't do those tasks especially fast, but they are so affordable that you can have an army of them. This hardware approach for GPUs was adopted because there's only so much improvement that can be made to the speed of individual cores. Even though the raw speed of cores increased with each generation, that wasn't nearly enough to close the performance gap to allow high-quality real-time rendering; the only solution was more cores.

CPUs, then, are great at tasks with steps that have to be completed in a specified order, like filling in a tax form. GPUs, though, are better at tasks that can be easily divided among many workers, like painting the outside of a house. Game renderers are designed to keep all of the GPU cores as busy as possible.

Why Games Don't Ray Trace

We saw in the preceding chapter how ray tracing can produce amazing graphics. But games don't ray trace, because it's too slow for real-time rendering. There are several reasons for this.

One reason is that ray tracing doesn't match up well with the "army of workers" GPU design. For example, ray tracing sends out a beam of light for each pixel, determines where that beam strikes, and from that point of impact, sends out a bunch more light beams, determines where they strike, and so on. This job is better suited for a CPU, because the renderer must determine each point of impact before it knows what beams to check next.

More broadly, realtime renders should expend computational effort where the result makes a difference to the viewer. Consider a computer-generated scene in which you face a chair in the middle of a polished wooden floor. A ray tracer, pinballing light around the room, would still indirectly determine the color of every point on the back of the chair, because that data is necessary for proper global illumination of the floor. A game renderer, though, could never afford the luxury of coloring a surface that won't be directly seen.

All Lines and No Curves

To understand how a video game renders without ray tracing, we start with the basic building block of game graphics: the triangle. In the previous chapter we learned how CGI models in movies are made of lines and curves. In game rendering, models are normally made exclusively of lines. If you remember graphing parabolas in high school algebra, you'll recall that the math for describing curves is a lot more complicated than the math for describing lines, and there's just not enough time to deal with curves in a game. That's why game renderers use lines, and this means that the surfaces defined by the control points are flat. The simplest flat surface is a triangle, defined by three points in space.

Triangles are ubiquitous in games. In a game, whatever you think you're looking at, you're actually looking at millions of triangles, joined at angles to create surfaces and shapes. Triangles used in rendering are often generically called *polygons*, even though almost all the polygons are simple triangles.

Games simulate curved surfaces by using lots and lots of triangles. A round tumbler, for example, can be approximated as a ring of interlocking triangles, as shown in Figure 5-1. On the right, the outlines of each triangle are shown for clarity.

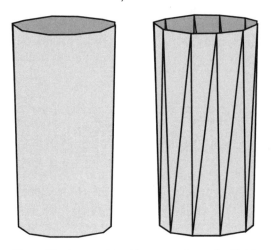

Figure 5-1: A curved tumbler approximated with triangles

Projection Without Ray Tracing

To render the triangles in the scene models, the renderer must project the control points that define the triangle to locate these points on the screen. Ray tracing projects by following an imaginary beam of light through the center of each pixel, but in this case we have to do something different.

The good news is that a direct mathematical relationship exists between world coordinates and screen coordinates, and this makes mapping the points fairly straightforward. We know the location—the x, y, and z world coordinates—of the viewpoint and of the point on the model we want to project. We also know the location of the virtual projection screen. Figure 5-2 shows how we use these locations to determine the exact y-coordinate where the line aimed at the model point crosses the projection screen. In this example, the depth (the distance from the viewpoint along the z-coordinate) of the projection screen is four-tenths of the depth from the viewpoint to the point on the model, as shown by the large blocks along the bottom. Knowing this proportion, we can calculate the x- and y-coordinates of the projected point. The y-coordinate of the projected point is four-tenths of the distance between the y-coordinate of the viewpoint and the y-coordinate of the point on the model, as shown by the shaded boxes on the projection screen. Also, though we can't see this from the perspective of Figure 5-2, the x-coordinate of the projected point will be four-tenths of the distance between the x-coordinates of the viewpoint and model point.

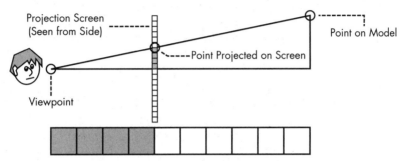

Figure 5-2: Projecting a point in the virtual world to the screen

Note that the position of the imaginary projection screen in the virtual world affects the resulting projection. To see this effect, make a rectangle using the forefinger and thumb of both hands and look through it while moving your hands close and then farther away. The farther away your hands are from your eyes, the narrower your *field of view*. In the same way, games can adjust field of view by altering the distance between the viewpoint and the projection screen in the virtual world. For example, games that let you look through binoculars or a gun scope accomplish the zoom effect by moving the projection screen deeper into the scene.

Rendering Triangles

With all three points of a triangle located in screen space, rendering a triangle follows the same rasterization process we saw in Chapter 4 to make a bitmap out of a 2D model. In Figure 5-3, the pixel centers inside the triangle boundaries are colored gray.

From reading the previous chapter, you probably have some objections to this simple method of triangle rendering. First, how can we just color every pixel the same—what about all those lighting effects? And second, look at those jaggies— how do we get rid of them?

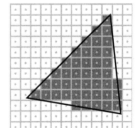

Figure 5-3: With the vertices of a triangle located on the screen, the triangle can be rendered.

These questions will be answered, but first we have to deal with a more fundamental problem. Simply determining where every triangle is located on the screen and coloring its pixels doesn't work because every pixel on the screen will probably be inside more than one triangle. Consider the image shown in Figure 5-4. The flowerpot is behind a cube, which is behind a tall cup. Pixel A lies within four different triangles: one on the front of the cup, one on the back of the cup, one on the front of the cube, and one on the side of the cube. Likewise, four triangles enclose pixel B. In each case, only one triangle should actually determine the color of the pixel. In order to render the image correctly, the renderer must always map each pixel to the model surface in the scene that is closest to the viewpoint. Ray tracing already finds the closest intersection point between the light beam and a model in the scene, so this problem is handled without any additional effort. Without ray tracing, though, what should the renderer do?

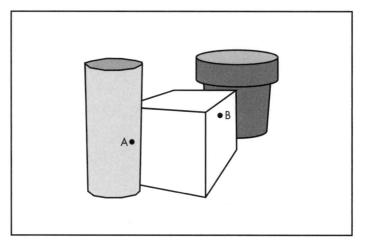

Figure 5-4: Three overlapping models in a scene

The Painter's Algorithm

A simple solution is known as the *painter's algorithm*. First, all of the triangles in the scene are ordered according to their distance from the viewpoint. Then the models are "painted" back to front, the way Bob Ross would paint a landscape on *The Joy of Painting*. This algorithm is easy for the programmer to implement, but it has several problems.

First, it's highly inefficient: the renderer will wind up coloring the same pixel over and over again as foreground models are rendered over previous background models, which is a huge waste of effort.

Second, it doesn't allow for easy subdivision to keep the army of workers busy on the GPU. The painter's algorithm requires the models to be drawn in a certain order, so it's difficult to effectively divide the work among separate processing units.

Third, there's not always an easy way to determine which of two triangles is farther way from the viewpoint. Figure 5-5 shows a perspective view of two triangles, with numbers indicating the depth of each vertex. The top view makes it clear which triangle is in front, but because the depths of one triangle's vertices are between those of the other triangle, there's no easy way to figure out which triangle is closer by direct comparison of the vertex depths.

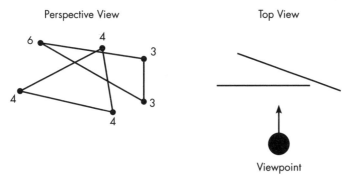

Perspective View

Top View

Figure 5-5: Perspective and top views of two triangles

Depth Buffering

Because of all the deficiencies of the painter's algorithm, the most common solution to projection in games is a method known as *depth buffering*. As introduced in the previous chapter, computer graphics require a bitmap called a display buffer to store the color of each pixel in a display. This technique also uses a corresponding *depth buffer* to track the depth of each pixel—how far away it is from the viewpoint. Of course, a screen is flat, so pixels don't really have depth. What the depth buffer actually stores is the depth of the point in the scene that was used to determine the color of that pixel. This allows the renderer to process the objects in the scene in any order.

Here's how depth buffering would work with the example scene from Figure 5-4. Initially, the depth of each pixel would be set to some maximal value that's greater than the depth of any actual object in the scene—let's say 100,000 virtual feet. If the cup is drawn first, the depth of those pixels in the depth buffer is set to the corresponding distances from the viewpoint. Suppose the flowerpot is drawn next; the renderer then sets the depth of its pixels. We can picture the depth buffer as a grayscale image, where pixels are darker the closer they are to the viewpoint. The depth buffer at this stage is shown in Figure 5-6.

The depth buffer solves the problem of projecting the right point onto the pixel. Before rendering a pixel, the renderer checks the depth buffer value for that pixel's location to see if the new pixel would be in front of or behind the pixel that's already in the display buffer. When a new pixel appears behind the pixel in that location in the display buffer, the renderer skips it and moves on. Continuing with our example, when the cube is drawn, the pixels on the left side of the cube that overlap with the cup are not drawn, because the values in the depth buffer show that the cup's pixels are in front of the cube. The cube would overwrite the pixels of the flowerpot, because the depth of the flowerpot pixels is greater than those of the cube.

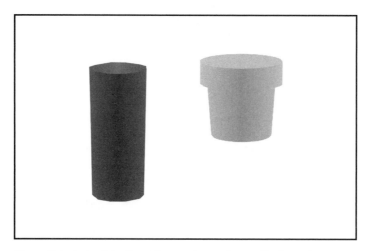

Figure 5-6: A depth buffer with two objects drawn. Darker colors are closer to the viewpoint.

Depth buffering is an efficient solution to projection because less work is thrown away. Models can be roughly preordered so that they are painted approximately front to back, to minimize overwritten pixels. Also, because depth buffers allow for rendering models in any order, work can more easily be divided among the cores of the graphics processor. In our example, different cores can be working on the cup, cube, and flowerpot at the same time, and the right model will be projected to each pixel in the final rendered image.

Real-Time Lighting

Now that the renderer knows which triangle each pixel belongs to, the pixel must be colored. In real-time rendering this is known as *pixel shading*. Once a particular pixel has passed the depth buffer test, all the data needed to color the pixel is processed by an algorithm called a pixel shader. Because each pixel can be independently colored, pixel shading is a great way to keep the army of workers busy inside the GPU.

The data needed by the shader will vary based on the complexity of the lighting model, including the location, direction, and color of the lights in the scene. Without a method like ray tracing, a full global illumination model, in which reflections from near surfaces color each other, isn't possible. However, shaders can include the basic effects of distance, diffuse reflections, and specular reflections.

In Figure 5-7, a beam of light represented by the solid arrow reflects from a triangle. The dashed arrow represents the *normal* (or *surface normal*) of the triangle in that location; a normal is simply a perpendicular line pointing away from the surface. In Chapter 4 we learned how the angles between light beams, surfaces, and viewpoints affect diffuse and specular reflections. The normal is used by the pixel shader for these calculations;

so, for example, in Figure 5-7, if the dark arrow represents a light beam, this would have high diffuse reflection because the angle between the light and the normal is small.

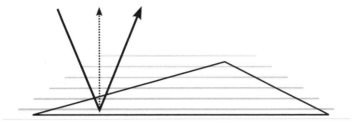

Figure 5-7: A triangle with a surface normal (dashed arrow) perpendicular to the triangle surface, and a light beam (dark arrow) striking the surface.

In Figure 5-7, the normal points straight up, meaning it is perpendicular to the plane of the triangle. Triangles with straight-up normals for every point on the surface are completely flat, which makes the individual triangles clearly visible in the rendering. For example, with straight-up normals, the tumbler in Figure 5-8 appears faceted like a gemstone.

For a more rounded appearance, the normals are bent as shown in Figure 5-9. Here, the normals at the corners are bent outward, and the normal at any location inside the triangle is a weighted average of the normals at the corner. Because the normal at the point of impact for the light beam no longer points straight up, the light beam reflects more sharply. If this were part of a diffuse lighting calculation, the resulting color would be brighter.

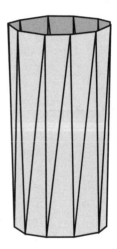

Figure 5-8: If the normals for each location on a triangle point the same way, this model will be rendered as a series of flat triangles.

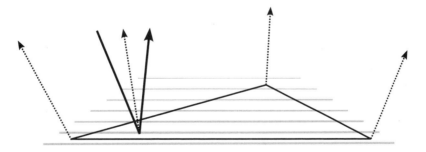

Figure 5-9: The normal at the point of light impact is affected by the bent corner normals, which changes the angle of reflection.

Bending normals allows the flat triangle to reflect light as though it were the bent triangle shown in Figure 5-10.

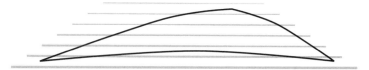

Figure 5-10: Bending the normals gives the triangle a bent shape so far as the lighting calculations are concerned.

This goes only so far in fixing the problem, though, because the underlying shape is unchanged. Bending normals doesn't affect which pixels are matched to which triangle; it affects only the lighting calculations in the pixel shader. Therefore, the illusion breaks down along the edges of a model. With our tumbler, bending normals helps the sides of the tumbler to appear smooth, but it doesn't affect the tumbler's silhouette, and the rim is still a series of straight lines. Smoother model renderings require additional techniques that we'll see later in this chapter.

Shadows

Shadowing plays an important part in convincing the viewer to accept the reality of an image by giving models weight and realism. Producing shadows requires tracing beams of light; a shadow is, after all, the outline of an object between a light source and a surface. Game renderers don't have time for full ray tracing, so they use clever shortcuts to produce convincing shadow effects.

Consider the scene outline shown in Figure 5-11. This scene will be rendered in a nighttime environment, so the lamppost on the left will cast strong shadows. To render the shadows properly, the renderer must determine which pixels visible from this viewpoint would be illuminated by the lamppost and which will be lit only by other light sources. In this example, the renderer must determine that the point labeled Scene-A is not visible from the lamppost, but Scene-B is.

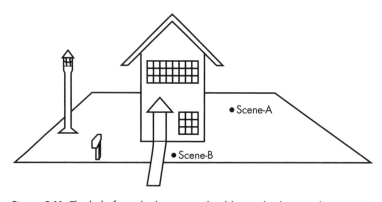

Figure 5-11: The light from the lamppost should cast shadows in this scene.

A common solution to this problem in games is a *shadow map*, a quickly rendered image from the point of view of a light source looking into the scene that calculates only the depth buffer, not the display buffer. Figure 5-12 is a shadow map for the lamppost in Figure 5-11, showing the distance from the lamppost to every point in the scene; as with the depth buffer, this is shown in grayscale with closer pixels colored darker.

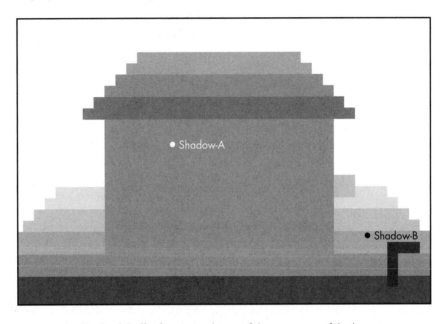

Figure 5-12: The depth buffer from a rendering of the viewpoint of the lamppost

Shadow maps are created for each light source before scene pixels are colored. When coloring a pixel, the pixel shader checks each light's shadow map to determine if the point being rendered is visible from that light. Consider the points Scene-A and Scene-B in Figure 5-11. The shader computes the distance from each of these points to the top of the lamppost and compares this distance to the depth of the same points projected onto the shadow map, labeled Shadow-A and Shadow-B in Figure 5-12. In this case, the depth of Shadow-A in Figure 5-12 is less than the distance between Scene-A and the lamppost in Figure 5-11, which means something is blocking that light from reaching Scene-A. In contrast, the depth of Shadow-B matches the distance from Scene-B to the lamppost. So Scene-A is in shadow, but Scene-B is not.

I deliberately gave the shadow map in Figure 5-12 a blocky appearance; to improve performance, shadow maps are often created at lower resolutions, making blocky shadows. If a game offers a "shadow quality" setting, this setting most likely controls the resolution of the shadow maps.

Ambient Light and Ambient Occlusion

The simpler lighting model in real-time rendering tends to produce images that are too dark. It's easy to overlook the effect of indirect lighting in the world around us. For example, standing outside in the daytime, you'll have enough light to read even if you stand in a solid shadow, because of indirect sunlight bouncing off nearby surfaces.

To produce images with natural-looking light levels, a game renderer will typically apply a simple *ambient light* model. This lighting is omnipresent, illuminating the surface of every model without regard to light beams or angles of incidence, so that even surfaces missed by in-scene lighting are not totally dark. Ambient lighting is used throughout games, even for indoor scenes. This is a situation where a little fakery produces a more realistic result.

Ambient lighting can also be used to adjust the mood of a scene. When you leave behind a golden, autumnal field to enter a dusky forest in an open-world game like *World of Warcraft*, a large part of the effect is the ambient lighting changing from bright yellow to dim blue.

Although the simple ambient lighting model keeps the rendering from being too dark, the method doesn't produce any shadows, which hurts a scene's realism. *Ambient occlusion* methods fake shadows from ambient light by following the observation that such shadows should occur in crevices, cracks, holes, and the like. Figure 5-13 shows the key idea. Point A is much less occluded than point B because the angle through which light can reach the point is much larger, letting more light through. Therefore, ambient light should have a greater influence on point A than point B.

For a renderer to measure the occlusion precisely, though, it would have to send out light beams in every direction, much like the scattering of light from diffuse lighting, but we already know that tracing light beams is not an option for real-time rendering. Instead, a technique called *screen space ambient occlusion (SSAO)* approximates the amount of occlusion for each pixel after the main rendering is over, using data that was already computed earlier in the rendering process.

In Figure 5-14 we see SSAO approximation in action. Note that the viewpoint is looking straight down at the surface. The dashed arrow is the normal for the point on the surface. The gray area is a hemisphere aligned with that normal, shown as a semicircle in this 2D representation. The shader examines a scattering of points inside the hemisphere. Each point is projected into screen coordinates, just like the projection of the model point shown back in Figure 5-2. Then the depth of the point is compared to he depth buffer for the pixel location, which tells the shader whether the point is in front of (shown in white) or behind (black) the model surface. The percentage of points behind the surface is a good approximation of the amount of ambient occlusion.

Viewpoint

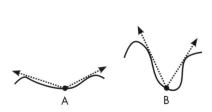

Figure 5-13: Measuring the occlusion at given points

Figure 5-14: Screen space ambient occlusion approximates the degree of occlusion by the percentage of points behind the model surface.

SSAO is heavy work for the renderer because it requires projecting and examining a lot of extra points—at least 16 per pixel for acceptable results. However, the calculations for each pixel are independent, which allows the work to be easily divided among the army of worker cores. If a gamer has the hardware to handle it, SSAO produces believable ambient shadowing.

Texture Mapping

Throughout these discussions of graphics, we have discussed models as though their surfaces were one solid color, but that describes few surfaces in the actual world. Tigers have stripes, rugs have patterns, wood has grain, and so on. To reproduce surfaces with complex coloring, pixel shaders employ *texture mapping*, which conceptually wraps a flat image onto the surface of a model, much like an advertising wrap on the side of a city bus. To be clear, texture mapping is not just for game rendering; movie CGI employs it extensively, too. But texture mapping is a special problem for games, in which textures have to be applied in milliseconds. The sheer number of textures and texture operations needed for a single frame presents one of the greatest challenges of game rendering.

Figure 5-15 shows a texture bitmap (an image of a zigzag pattern) and a scene in which the pattern has been applied. Bitmap images used for texture mapping are called *textures*. In this case, the surface of the rug rectangle is covered by a single large texture, although for regular patterns like the one on this rug, a smaller texture can be applied repeatedly to tile the surface.

The pixel shader is responsible for choosing the base color of the pixel using the associated texture; this base color is later modified by the lighting model. Because the textured surface is an arbitrary distance from the viewpoint, and at an arbitrary orientation, there's not a one-to-one correspondence between pixels in the texture and pixels on the model's surface. Choosing pixel colors in a textured area based on the applied texture is known as *sampling*.

Texture Bitmap

Texture Applied to Surface in Scene

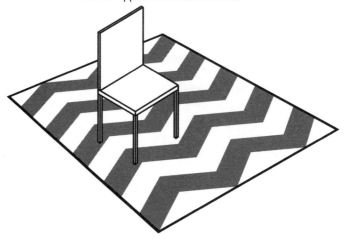

Figure 5-15: Texture mapping. The zigzag texture on top is applied to the rug object under the chair.

To illustrate the decisions involved in sampling, let's start with a bitmap of a robot with a hat, shown in Figure 5-16. The pixels in a texture are called *texels*. This 20×20 texture has 400 texels.

In this example, this texture will appear as a painting in the frame on the wall in Figure 5-17.

Suppose that the area inside the frame fills a 10×10 block of pixels in the rendered image. The texture will be applied head-on without any adjustment for perspective, which means all the renderer has to do is shrink the 20×20 block of texels to fit the 10×10 block of pixels in the final image.

Figure 5-16: A texture of a robot wearing a hat

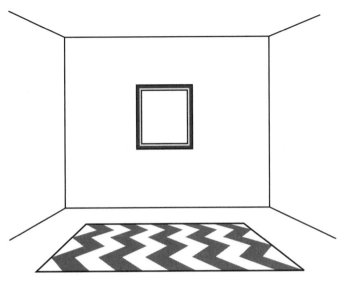

Figure 5-17: In this scene, the texture of Figure 5-16 will be applied inside the picture frame on the wall.

Nearest-Neighbor Sampling

Because 10×10 pixels are needed to fill the textured area, let's imagine a grid of 100 sample points overlaying the texture. Figure 5-18 shows a close-up section of the original robot texture from Figure 5-16. Here, the centers of the texels are shown as squares, and the crosses represent the sample points for the pixels in the scene. Sampling resolves this mismatch of pixels to texels.

The simplest method of sampling is choosing the color of the nearest texel, an approach known as *nearest-neighbor sampling*. This approach is easy to implement and fast to compute, but tends to look horrible. In this example, each of four texels is equally close to the pixel centers, so I've arbitrarily chosen the texel in the lower right of each pixel center. Figure 5-19 shows the texels chosen by this sampling method, and the 10×10-pixel block that would appear in the final image.

As you can see, the result looks more like a skeletal aerobics instructor than a robot with a hat. If you've ever looked closely at an oil painting, you may guess why the nearest-neighbor technique produces such an unattractive result. Up close, an oil painting reveals a wealth of detail, a multitude of individual brushstrokes. Take a few steps back, though, and the strokes vanish as the colors blend together in the eye. In the same way, when a texture is represented with fewer pixels, the colors of neighboring texels should blend. Nearest-neighbor sampling, though, simply picks the color of one texel with no blending; in our example, three out of four texels have no influence on the result at all.

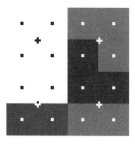

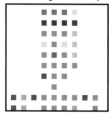

Figure 5-18: A close-up section of
the Figure 5-16 texture. Squares
are texel centers; crosses are
sample points.

Figure 5-19: The result of 10×10 nearest-
neighbor sampling on Figure 5-16. On the
left are the selected texels of the original texture, and on the right is the resulting bitmap.

When a texture is expanded to
fill a larger area, the results are just as
ugly. In this case, some of the texels
will simply be repeated in the textured
area, producing a blocky result. To see
the problem, let's start with a triangle
and its representation as a 16×16 anti-
aliased texture, as shown in Figure 5-20.

Now suppose this texture is applied
over a 32×32 area. Ideally, it should look
smoother than the original, smaller texture; the greater resolution offers the
opportunity for a finer edge. As shown
in Figure 5-21, though, nearest-neighbor sampling puts four sample points
in each texel, so every texel in the original 16×16 texture simply becomes
four identically colored pixels at the larger size.

Triangle

16×16 Triangle
Bitmap

Figure 5-20: A triangle and its representation as an anti-aliased 16×16-
pixel texture.

Nearest Neighbor Sampling

32×32 Bitmap Results

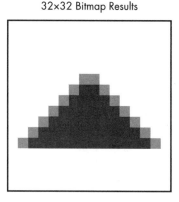

Figure 5-21: When used to enlarge textures, nearest-neighbor sampling
merely duplicates pixels.

Bilinear Filtering

A better-looking sampling method is *bilinear filtering*. Instead of taking the color of the nearest texel, each texture sample is a proportional blend of the four nearest texels. The method is called bilinear because it uses the position of the sample point along two axes within the square formed by the four nearest texels. For example, in Figure 5-22, the sample point toward the bottom and just left of center results in the mixing percentages shown. The final color of this sample is computed from the colors of the texels at the given percentages.

Figure 5-23 shows the robot texture after reduction via bilinear filtering. With only a fourth of the original pixels, the reduced version necessarily lacks detail, but if you hold the original at arm's length and compare to the reduced version held close, you'll see the reduction is a good representation, and much better than the nearest-neighbor result.

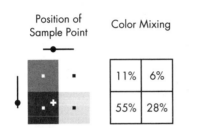

Position of Sample Point   Color Mixing

| 11% | 6% |
| 55% | 28% |

Figure 5-22: Bilinear filtering measures the position of a sample point vertically and horizontally within the square of neighboring texels, and uses these positions to determine the percentage that each texel influences the sample color.

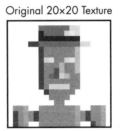

Original 20×20 Texture   Bilinear Filtered 10×10 Bitmap

Figure 5-23: The robot texture reduced through bilinear filtering

Figure 5-24 shows a 32×32 area blown up from the 16×16 triangle texture using bilinear filtering—a clear improvement over the chunky nearest-neighbor sampling.

Original 16×16 Texture   Bilinear Filtered 32×32 Bitmap

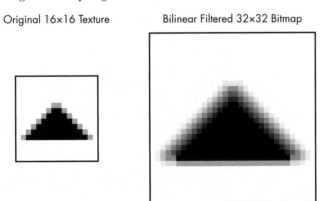

Figure 5-24: The triangle texture expanded through bilinear filtering

Mipmaps

The examples in the previous section show the limit of what is possible with bilinear filtering. For bilinear filtering to look good, the texture needs to be at least half, but no more than twice, the resolution of the textured area. If the texture is any smaller, bilinear filtering still produces blocky results. If the texture is too large, even though four texels are used per sample, some texels won't contribute to any samples.

Avoiding these problems requires a set of different-sized bitmaps for each texture: a large, full-resolution version for viewing up close, and smaller versions for when the textured area is also small. This collection of progressively smaller textures is known as a *mipmap*. An example is shown in Figure 5-25. Each texture in the mipmap is one-quarter of the area of the next larger texture.

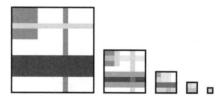

Figure 5-25: A mipmap is a collection of textures, each one-quarter the size of the previous.

With a mipmap, the renderer can always find a texture that will produce good results with bilinear filtering. If a 110×110 texture is needed, for example, the 128×128 texture is shrunk. If a 70×70 texture is required, the 64×64 texture is magnified.

Trilinear Filtering

While bilinear filtering and mipmaps work reasonably well, they introduce a distracting visual anomaly when transitioning from one mipmap texture to another. Suppose, in a first-person game, you're running toward a brick wall that uses a mipmapped texture. As you get closer to the wall, the smaller texture will get blown up more and more until you reach the point where you get a shrunk-down version of the next larger texture in the mipmap. Unfortunately, a larger texture that has been reduced through bilinear filtering doesn't quite match a smaller version of the same texture that has been expanded, so at the moment of this transition the texture will "pop." The problem can also occur with no movement at all on a surface that stretches out to the distance, such as a long rug in a corridor, that has been tiled with a repeating texture; because the parts of rug at different distances are covered by different textures in the mipmap, seams will be clearly visible where the textures touch.

To smooth over the texture transition, the renderer can blend samples from different textures in addition to blending between texels in a texture. Suppose the area to be textured is 70×70, a size that falls between the 64×64 and 128×128 textures in a mipmap. Instead of just using bilinear filtering on the nearer-sized 64×64 texture, the renderer can use bilinear filtering on both the larger and smaller textures, then blend the two resulting samples. As with the bilinear filtering itself, this final step is proportional: in our example, the color would be mostly determined by the result from the 64×64 texture, with a little of the 128×128 result mixed in. Because we are filtering in two dimensions on each texture, then blending the results, this technique is known as *trilinear filtering*. It is demonstrated in Figure 5-26.

Trilinear filtering eliminates popping and seaming between textures in a mipmap, but because it requires two bilinear samples and then a final blend, it does over twice as much work as bilinear filtering.

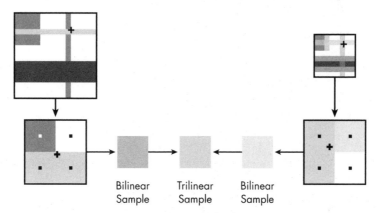

Bilinear   Trilinear   Bilinear
Sample   Sample   Sample

Figure 5-26: Trilinear filtering takes bilinear samples from the larger and smaller textures in a mipmap and blends the results.

Reflections

As discussed in Chapter 4, ray tracing naturally captures all the effects of light reflecting from one surface to another. Unfortunately, the subtle influence of colors of nearby surfaces is nearly impossible to capture without ray tracing, but game renderers do have a way to fake what I'll call *clear reflections*: the more obvious, mirror-like reflections on such surfaces as polished countertops, windows, and of course mirrors themselves.

Games limit which surfaces produce clear reflections. Having just a few objects with such reflections maintains the realism of the scene at a much lower computational cost. To reduce the workload further, renderers use *environment mapping*, in which shiny objects are conceptually placed inside cubes that are texture-mapped with a previously rendered image of the object's surroundings.

Figure 5-27 shows a sample situation: a shiny sports car on a showroom turntable. To compute the effect of clear reflections, the renderer conceptually places the car in a cube; the cube itself is not rendered, but used only to map reflections. The inside of the cube is texture-mapped with an image of the showroom interior, as shown in Figure 5-28. Because the reflected images will be somewhat distorted anyway by the surface of the car body, viewers won't notice that the reflections don't perfectly match the rendered world in which the car is placed.

Figure 5-27: For realism, the shiny car body should reflect the showroom.

Figure 5-28: For the purpose of mapping reflections, the car is considered to be in a cube, the insides of which are covered by a bitmap image of the showroom.

Instead of tracing light as it pinballs around the scene, mapping reflections becomes an indirect texture-map reference, a relatively simple calculation. Of course, the surface of the car is probably also texture-mapped, which means that adding reflections is at least doubling the per-pixel effort, but the gain in realism is usually worth the extra work.

The job becomes harder when a reflecting model is moving, as would happen if our car were racing down a desert road in a driving game. The renderer can't simply paste a static image of a desert inside a cube and expect this to fool the viewer. Because the viewpoint will be moving with the car as the car travels down the road, the reflections must likewise travel— or at least give that appearance.

There's an old Hollywood trick that was used to convey the illusion of sideways movement in relation to the camera. An actor would stand on a treadmill so he could walk without going anywhere. Behind him an illustration of scenery on a continuous roll would slide past at the same speed as the treadmill. As long as the audience didn't notice the same trees going by, it looked as though the actor was actually moving sideways.

The same idea can be applied inside the cube around the shiny car. A portion of a wide continuous image is selected, as shown in Figure 5-29. Sliding the selection "window" across the wide image to match the movement of the car creates the illusion that the car is reflecting the arid mountains depicted in the scene.

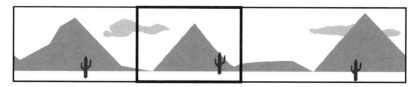

Figure 5-29: Sliding a window down a wide, continuous image creates the effect of movement in mapped reflections.

Faking Curves

Nothing in a video game destroys realism faster than a model with easily recognizable triangles trying to represent a rounded shape. Early 3D games were filled with car tires shaped like octagons and human characters that looked like they were made of toy bricks. We've already seen one part of the solution to this problem—bending the normals of triangle vertices—but producing smooth models requires a whole set of techniques.

Distant Impostors

An obvious solution to the problem of flat triangles is to break models down into so many small triangles that the individual facets are too small to be recognized. That works in theory, but even though triangles are simple shapes, there's still a limit to how many can be rendered in the time allowed. Trying to design each model at the highest possible detail would slow rendering to a crawl.

A renderer could, however, use lots of extra triangles to smooth out just those models closest to the viewpoint. This is the idea behind *distant impostors*. Here, each object in a game is modeled twice—a fully detailed high-triangle model and a simplified model with relatively few triangles. This simplified model is the "impostor" of the original, and is swapped in for the high-quality model whenever the model gets beyond a certain distance from the viewpoint.

Distant impostors make effective use of rendering time, but because the two models are so dissimilar, if a player is watching a particular model while moving closer to it, the transition between the models can be visually jarring. Ideally, you'd like to give the viewer the feeling that the distant object is revealing greater detail as it comes closer, but in practice the two models are so different that the replacement looks like one object magically transforming into another.

Bump Mapping

Another technique for smoothing models keeps the triangle count the same, but alters the lighting calculations at each pixel to give the appearance of an irregular surface.

To understand why this *bump mapping* method can be so effective, imagine a game featuring a hacienda with stucco walls. To get the appearance of stucco, the renderer can apply a texture made from an image of an actual stucco wall to the walls of the hacienda model. Because stucco is wavy, its undulations should be visible under the scene lighting. Merely applying a texture to a flat wall wouldn't convince the eye; it would look like a flat wall with a picture of stucco on it.

Bump mapping allows flat surfaces to react to light as though they were wavy like stucco, bumpy like popcorn ceilings, crumpled, louvered, or anything else. The process starts with a grayscale bitmap the same size as the texture that will be applied to the model surface. This bitmap is known as a *height map*, because the brightness of each pixel indicates the height of the surface.

The height map allows a pixel shader to approximate the surface normal at each pixel location. This is easiest to understand in 2D. Figure 5-30 shows a row of 10 pixels. The numbers at the bottom represent the height of each pixel. The 10 points are shown at proportionate heights, along with the surface normals. I've added gray lines to show how the normals for the fourth and seventh points are computed. An imaginary line is drawn between the two points on either side of a chosen point; then, the normal for the chosen point is set perpendicular to this line.

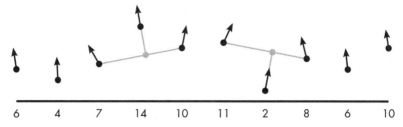

| 6 | 4 | 7 | 14 | 10 | 11 | 2 | 8 | 6 | 10 |

Figure 5-30: A row of pixels with light calculations altered by bump mapping. The numbers indicate the artificial height of each pixel. The renderer determines the normal at each pixel based on the heights of neighboring pixels.

These bent normals affect the calculations for both diffuse and specular lighting, allowing a flat surface to react to light as though it were rough or wavy. As with previous tricks that involved bending normals, though, a surface with a bump map is still a flat surface. The points on the surface are not actually raised or lowered, but merely react to light as though they were pointing in different directions. As a player moving through a 3D scene passes a bump-mapped model, the lighting on the surface will change in a realistic manner, but the edges of the model will still be straight, possibly giving the game away. Just as the rim of the tumbler back in Figure 5-8 betrayed the straight lines on the model, the outside corners of our bump-mapped hacienda will be perfectly straight when they should be wavy, because bump mapping doesn't alter the shape of the flat wall.

Tessellation

Suppose you're playing a fantasy game, and all your attention is focused on a huge ogre slowly approaching with an axe in his hands. As a gamer, you want this ogre to look as good as possible even as he gets close enough to nearly fill the screen, but you don't want him made out of so many triangles that the frame rate is too low for you to effectively fight him.

If the renderer uses a distant impostor, though, there will be a jarring transition that will remind you that you're just playing a game. If the renderer bump-maps the ogre model, the light will reflect realistically off the rivets in his armor, but the neat lighting effect won't hide the fact that the model just has too few triangles to be viewed up close.

A process known as *tessellation* solves this problem. First, each triangle in the ogre model is subdivided into more triangles. The corners of these new triangles are then manipulated independently inward or outward (that is, up or down in relation to the original triangle) using a height map. Instead of merely bending normals to trick the lighting model as bump mapping does, tessellation actually produces a model with more detail. Figure 5-31 demonstrates the process for a single triangle.

This method is a great way to cover up the straight lines of triangles and is a clear improvement in appearance over bump mapping and distant impostors. Because the model is actually deformed into a new, more complicated shape, even the edges of the model are properly affected, unlike with bump mapping. Also, unlike the distant impostor technique, the model improves gradually as the distance from the viewpoint decreases, avoiding the sharp transition when models are swapped.

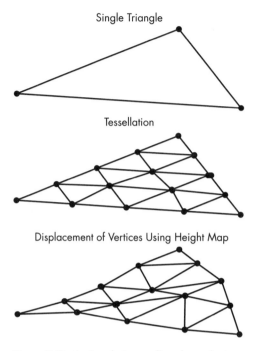

Figure 5-31: A triangle is tessellated, producing a web of smaller triangles. These new triangle vertices are then manipulated using a height map to produce the more complex surface on the bottom.

Though you might think that tessellation is used extensively in games, it's not, because it inflicts a much larger performance hit than the simpler methods discussed earlier. Creating more complex models on the fly is a lot more work than accessing one of several premade models as in the distant impostor method, or adjusting normals in bump mapping.

Tessellation is therefore used where the results are most obvious. For example, in a game set outdoors, the ground beneath the avatar's feet may stretch far into the distance. Modeling the ground in great detail would require a huge number of triangles, creating a performance bottleneck, but if the ground model has a low triangle count, the ground closest to the viewer will have an unrealistic, angular appearance. Tessellation can smooth out just the closest part of the ground.

Anti-Aliasing in Real Time

All of the renderer's hard work can go down the drain if individual pixels become clearly visible through aliasing. As with movie CGI, games need some form of full-screen anti-aliasing to smooth over the edges of models and surfaces. With ray tracing, anti-aliasing is conceptually simple: send out more beams than pixels and blend the results. Game renderers, though, must use more efficient techniques.

Supersampling

The most direct approximation to casting multiple beams is known as *supersampling anti-aliasing (SSAA)*. Instead of casting multiple beams per pixel, supersampling renders an intermediate image that is much larger than the desired final image. The color of each pixel in the final image is a blend of a sample of pixels from the larger image.

Consider the two white triangles covered by a gray triangle shown in Figure 5-32. Note that the edges of the white triangles won't be visible in the rendered image but are shown here for clarity.

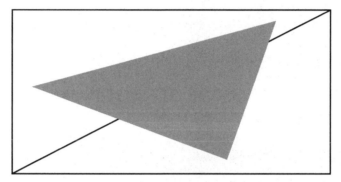

Figure 5-32: An arrangement of three triangles

Figure 5-33 demonstrates a basic rendering of these triangles at an 8×4 resolution. Each pixel is colored gray or white depending on whether the pixel center lies within the area of the gray triangle in the foreground.

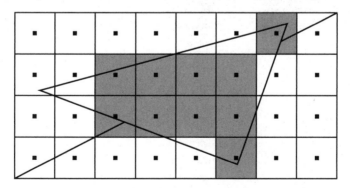

Figure 5-33: Coloring pixels without anti-aliasing

To produce an 8×4 supersampled image, the triangles are first rendered at a 16×8 resolution as shown in Figure 5-34.

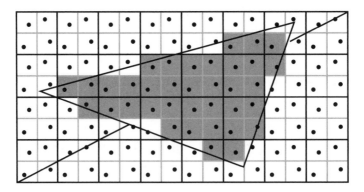

Figure 5-34: Supersampling the three triangles. Here, each pixel in the final bitmap is represented by four subpixels with scattered sample points.

As you can see, each pixel in Figure 5-33 has become four smaller pixels in Figure 5-34. These smaller pixels are called *subpixels*. Using this higher-resolution rendering, the color of each pixel in the final rendering is a proportional blend of the colors of its four subpixels, as shown in Figure 5-35.

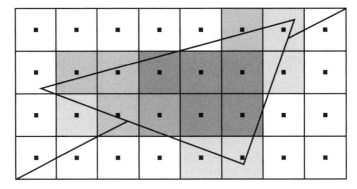

Figure 5-35: Coloring each pixel by blending subpixels

Supersampling does a nice job of smoothing out the jaggies, but as you might expect, rendering the image at a much higher resolution incurs a large performance penalty. Sampling four pixels to make one pixel in the final image is four times as much work for the pixel shader. In this example, I've kept things simple by assigning a flat color to each triangle, but in a typical game render each subpixel represents, at a minimum, a texture map sample followed by lighting calculations. Although earlier generations of video games commonly used SSAA, it's rare to see this method now.

Multisampling

In the previous example you can see that when all four subpixels are inside the same triangle, supersampling doesn't accomplish anything. To reduce the performance hit of anti-aliasing, the subpixel work can be limited to the edges of triangles where the jaggies occur, a technique known as *multisample anti-aliasing (MSAA)*.

Figure 5-36 demonstrates one version of this concept. Two pixels lie across the edge between two triangles. With supersampling, each of the eight subpixels is texture-sampled and individually colored by scene lighting. With multisampling, there are still eight subpixels for the two pixels, but not eight samples. Instead, the renderer first determines which triangle contains each subpixel. Each of the four subpixels that lie within the same triangle is given the same color, which has been sampled from a point midway between the subpixel sample points. So while supersampling colors eight subpixels A through H, multisampling colors only four subpixels A through D, which means substantially less work in texture mapping and lighting.

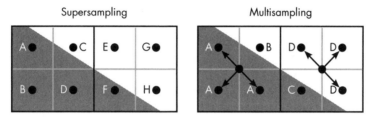

Figure 5-36: Comparing supersampling and multisampling

When all four subpixels lie within the interior of the same triangle, multisampling colors only one subpixel per final pixel, introducing little computational overhead. Multisampling puts in extra effort where it is most needed—reducing jaggies at edges—and thus is an efficient use of rendering time.

Post-Process Anti-Aliasing

Performance can be improved even further by delaying anti-aliasing until the image is rendered, an idea known as *post-process anti-aliasing*. That is, the image is first rendered normally at the desired final resolution, and then the jaggies are identified and smoothed over. In essence, a post-process anti-aliasing technique decides that some of the pixels in an image are colored incorrectly based on nothing more than the colors of the pixels themselves.

One such method is called *fast approximate anti-aliasing*, or *FXAA*. (Why that wouldn't be FAAA is perhaps a question we're not supposed to ask.) The idea behind FXAA is to find pixels that are likely to be along the edge between overlapping triangles, and then blend neighboring pixel colors to smooth the jarring transition.

FXAA examines each pixel in the image separately—let's call the pixel under examination the *current* pixel. The process starts by computing the perceived brightness of the current pixel and its four immediate neighbors, similar to examining a black-and-white version of the image. The brightest and dimmest pixels in the neighborhood are selected, as shown in Figure 5-37, and their difference is compared to a cut-off value. This test ensures that the anti-aliasing is applied only to pixel neighborhoods of high contrast—areas where the difference between the brightest and dimmest pixels is large.

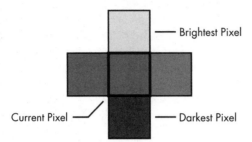

Figure 5-37: Checking the level of contrast in a pixel's neighborhood

These high-contrast areas likely represent jagged edges that need to be smoothed, and each such area is further examined as shown in Figure 5-38. The 3×3 block of pixels centered on the current pixel is considered both as a set of three columns and a set of three rows to determine whether this is a horizontal or vertical edge. In this example, because the columns are similar to each other but one row strongly contrasts with the other two, this would be classified as a horizontal edge.

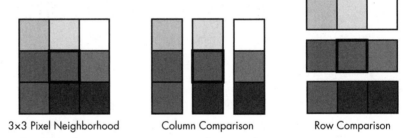

3×3 Pixel Neighborhood   Column Comparison   Row Comparison

Figure 5-38: Looking for contrast in the columns and rows of a pixel neighborhood

Because this is a horizontal edge, the next step is to compare the pixels above and below the current pixel to find which contrasts the most with the current pixel. In this case, the pixel above is much brighter than the current pixel, while the pixel below is quite similar. This means the detected edge is between the current pixel and its topside neighbor. To anti-alias this edge, the current pixel will be replaced by a bilinear sample between the pixel centers, shown as the white circle in Figure 5-39. FXAA examines other pixels along the edge to determine how jagged

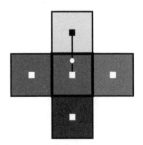

Figure 5-39: To smooth this edge, FXAA will replace the color of the center pixel with a bilinear sample at the circle point.

the edge is, adjusting the degree of blending by placing the sample point farther from the center of the current pixel.

A post-process anti-aliasing method like FXAA is very fast compared to supersampling or even multisampling because it doesn't create any sub-pixels at all. However, the results of FXAA are not always as impressive as other methods. In particular, FXAA can sometimes blur areas that weren't actually aliased; unlike supersampling, post-process methods like FXAA are only guessing where the edges are, so areas of high contrast within textures may fool the algorithm.

The Rendering Budget

The trade-offs that accompany different anti-aliasing techniques mean that developers of real-time graphics applications must choose between best quality and best performance. Is FXAA good enough for this situation? Or is MSAA necessary? This choice, though, is not made in isolation. More broadly, game developers must review all the techniques available for real-time rendering—lighting and shadows and anti-aliasing, and lots of other possibilities we don't have the space to discuss, like motion blur and particle systems—and select a set that maximizes the quality of the images without exceeding the time allowed for rendering. Within that $1/60$ of a second, a surprising amount of work can be done, but all of the best-looking techniques can't be used, so sacrifices have to be made somewhere.

On a console or in a mobile game, these choices are usually all made by the game designer. On PCs, a degree of choice is usually afforded to the user, who is given controls to raise or lower the resolution of textures, select the method of texture filtering, choose among anti-aliasing methods, turn shadows and reflections on or off, and tweak the renderer in a host of other ways. In part, this control is given so the user can adjust the render workload to match the performance of the particular system, since the PC in question might be top of the line, or an aging clunker.

Beyond that, though, detailed rendering options reflect the truth that beauty is subjective: what impresses one viewer might have no effect on another. Some gamers are horrified by jagged edges, for example, and always crank up anti-aliasing to the maximum, while others wouldn't dream of devoting precious processor cycles to removing jaggies when there are more realistic shadows to be had instead. In a sense, video games are all about placing ourselves inside believable illusions, and what we believe is up to us.

What's Next for Game Graphics

So where do game graphics go from here? We can expect game programmers to continue to be challenged by advancements in displays. Monitors keep increasing in resolution, eating away some of the benefit of each new GPU generation. A special challenge will come from virtual reality (VR) headsets, which combine displays mounted inside helmets with sensors to track the gamer's head movements. VR headsets can be trouble if the display lags behind the movement—our brains don't like conflicting information, and when our eyes are saying one thing, and our inner ear something else, the result for many people is nausea. In a game played on a normal flat screen, gamers would prefer a consistently high frame rate but don't get too bent out of shape by sporadic dips in the number; with VR devices, an absolutely rock-steady frame rate is imperative.

Beyond matching the needs of displays, it's difficult to predict exactly how game graphics will progress. Over the past decade, every time I've played a new AAA game (as the industry calls the biggest-budget titles), I find myself thinking the graphics can't get any better, that whatever improvements the next generation of hardware brings will be insignificant. And every time, I've been proven wrong. So I'm confident that I'll continue to be blown away by the advances in game graphics, even if I can't be sure what those advances will be.

Raw hardware power is only part of the equation. Buying a new GPU with twice as many cores as an older GPU means the hardware can process twice as many triangles in the same allotment of time, but once triangle counts get high enough, doubling them doesn't improve the resulting images very much. Indeed, at some point, models may get so detailed and triangle counts so high that the average triangle will occupy less than a one-pixel area on the screen. When that happens, it will call into question the whole idea of rendering the scene as a series of triangles. Rather than projecting three triangle vertices to determine the color of one pixel, renderers may replace triangles with single points of fixed volume—imagine building a sculpture out of tiny marshmallows.

What ultimately drives advancements in game graphics, though, isn't hardware, but the creativity of graphics programmers. Many of the techniques in Chapter 4 are about making accurate, or at least plausible, simulations of how light and vision work in the real world. Game graphics are just about making results that look good. That gives programmers enormous leeway to experiment, to find new ways to spend part of the precious rendering budget, to find new tricks to put silly grins on the faces of gamers. I don't know for sure what game developers are cooking up for the next generation of games, but I'm sure that they'll continue to put my GPU to work in ways that will thrill and amaze.

6

DATA COMPRESSION

Sometimes the hard work of software is obvious to everyone, as it is with movie CGI and video game graphics. You don't have to know anything about how computers work to be impressed with the visuals in films like *Avatar* and games like *Crysis*. Sometimes, though, software is doing its most amazing work when it looks like it's not working hard at all.

Watching a high-definition movie on a disc or streamed over the Internet is something most of us take for granted. Isn't that just storing and displaying images? Why would that require special techniques? To understand why we should be impressed with Blu-ray video and Netflix streaming, let's look at what video was like before these formats came to be.

Videocassettes, the earliest home video medium, recorded images on a roll of magnetic tape. These were analog recordings—magnetic transcriptions of the same signal that would've been broadcast by television antennas. The video resolution was even lower than what we now call "standard definition," and as with other analog recordings like audiocassettes and vinyl records, the quality of the video would degrade over time. The one upside to videocassettes was their capacity: a longer movie merely required a longer spool of tape.

Next came the LaserDisc. About the size of LP records, these discs looked like larger versions of today's DVDs and Blu-ray discs, but like videocassettes, they were still storing the analog broadcast-format signal. However, LaserDiscs recorded a higher-resolution picture that came close to standard definition, and allowed you to jump to particular places in the video without having to rewind or fast-forward the way you would with a videocassette. For a while, the LaserDisc seemed like the future of video, but now capacity was a problem. Unlike the effectively limitless capacity of a magnetic tape roll, LaserDiscs could hold only 60 minutes of video per side, so watching a movie meant flipping the disc halfway through or even switching discs.

Today, the problem of capacity is even more serious. Our Blu-ray discs are much smaller than LaserDiscs, but our videos are a much higher resolution. Let me put the problem into numbers. In high-definition video each frame is a 1920×1080 bitmap, a total of 2,073,600 pixels. If each pixel is stored in three-byte RGB format, one frame of a high-definition movie would require 6,220,800 bytes, or about 6.2 megabytes (*mega* means "million"). Movies are recorded at 24 or 30 frames per second, which is 1,800 frames per minute, 108,000 frames per hour, or 216,000 frames for a two-hour film. If each frame is 6,220,800 bytes, then 216,000 frames is 1,343,693 megabytes, or about 1,345 gigabytes (*giga* means "billion").

How can all of that data fit on a Blu-ray disc? Part of the answer is the "blu-ray" itself, a blue laser that's narrower than the laser used on LaserDiscs or even conventional DVDs, allowing more data to be packed into a smaller area, just as smaller print allows more words on a page. Even so, a Blu-ray can store only about 50 gigabytes(GB) of data, less than 4 percent of what's required.

Streaming video has the same problem. If one frame of video is 6.2 megabytes (MB), and the video is running at 30 frames per second, then streaming requires an Internet connection of 186 megabytes per second (MBps). A typical home broadband connection is more like 4MBps. What's worse, because of traffic congestion and hiccups in the network, you can't count on maintaining the full rated bandwidth over the course of a long transmission. Realistically, streaming video should use no more than a couple of MBps at most.

So how can we fit giant amounts of video data into these small containers? The answer is *data compression*—storing data in a format that requires fewer bytes than the original format. Compression techniques can be broadly divided into two categories. With *lossless compression*, the compressed data can be restored to its exact original state. In contrast, *lossy compression* accepts that the restored data may be slightly different than the original. Video streaming and storage uses a combination of both types of compression. In this chapter, we'll first investigate some general compression techniques using simple examples. Then we'll see how these ideas apply to video, producing highly compressed sequences of images that look nearly as good as the uncompressed originals.

Run-Length Encoding

Most of us have employed some form of lossless compression, though we wouldn't have called it that, because many techniques for lossless compression are commonsense ideas. One such method is *run-length encoding.* Suppose I were to show you a 27-digit number for one minute to see whether you could remember it an hour later. That might sound hard, but look at the number:

777,777,777,555,555,555,222,222,222

I suspect you wouldn't try to remember each digit individually. Instead, you'd count the occurrences of each digit, and remember it as "nine sevens, nine fives, and nine twos."

That's run-length encoding in action. Repeats of the same piece of data (in this case, a digit) are called *runs*, and when runs are common, we can shorten the data by recording the lengths of the runs rather than the whole number. Run-length encoding is lossless compression, because if we remember the shorthand version of the number, we can reproduce the number in its original form whenever needed.

Just by itself, run-length encoding can provide excellent compression for certain types of images, such as icons, logos, comic-book-style illustrations— any image with large blocks of solid color. When pixels have the same color as their neighbors, we can reduce the storage requirements considerably. As an example, I'll describe the system used by the *TGA* image file format. TGA is short for *Truevision Graphics Adapter,* an early piece of graphics hardware designed for video editors. The file format, if not the adapter, is still in use in the video industry, and is probably the simplest example of run-length encoding for images.

The image data in a TGA file is compressed on a row-by-row basis. Within each row, each run of two or more pixels of exactly the same color is identified. The remaining pixels are called *raw* pixels. Consider the selected row in the sample image in Figure 6-1. In this row, there are several short runs of pixels, and several raw pixels that are different from their neighbors.

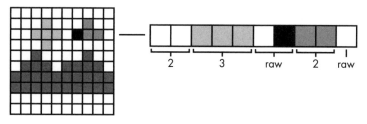

Figure 6-1: The selected row has a mix of runs and raw pixels.

The TGA format organizes runs and raw pixels into *packets*. Each packet begins with a one-byte header. The leftmost bit of the header byte determines whether it is a run packet or a raw packet. The other seven bits denote the size of the packet in pixels. Because the smallest packet has one pixel, TGA encodes the packet's size as one less than its actual size; that is, a size field of 0000000 represents a size of 1, and 0000001 represents 2, and so on. Following the header is either the encoded color of all the pixels in the run, or for a raw packet, the colors of each individual pixel. Using the RGB color format, the row of pixels from Figure 6-1 would be encoded as shown in Table 6-1.

Table 6-1: TGA Encoding of Pixel Row

Run/raw	Size	Red	Green	Blue	Description
1	0000001	11111111	11111111	11111111	Run of two white pixels
1	0000010	11001100	11001100	00000000	Run of three yellow pixels
0	0000001	11111111	11111111	11111111	Raw packet of two pixels; first is white
		00000000	10000000	00000000	Second pixel in raw packet; dark green
1	0000001	00000000	00000000	11111111	Run of two blue pixels
0	0000000	11111111	11111111	11111111	One raw white pixel

This encoding requires 23 bytes versus the uncompressed size of 30 bytes. This *compression ratio* of 30:23, or about 4:3, isn't very high, but note that a mere 4 bytes are needed to store rows where every pixel is the same color, like the top row of Figure 6-1. The overall compression ratio of this bitmap in TGA format is an impressive 300:114, or about 5:2.

Dictionary Compression

Just by itself, run-length encoding can compress pictures with large blocks of solid colors, but most of the images in movies aren't like that. For photographs and other types of digital images with lots of color variation, software has to work much harder to find patterns exploitable by compression. One of the key tools is known as *dictionary compression.*

The Basic Method

Later we'll see how dictionary compression is used on images, but the idea is easiest to understand when it is applied to a text document, so let's start there. An uncompressed text document is stored as a series of character codes such as ASCII.

We'll compress this sample paragraph:

> Those pictures created by a computer are called computer graphics. When these pictures created by the computer are viewed in a sequence, that sequence is called an animation. An entire movie created from an animation, a sequence of pictures created by a computer, is called a computer-animated movie.

To make this example simpler, I'll ignore the spaces and punctuation in this text and just worry about the letters. There are 234 letters in this paragraph; stored as uncompressed ASCII text, the letters would require 234 bytes. To employ dictionary compression on this text, we first need a *dictionary*, which in this context is a numbered list of every word in the document being compressed. Table 6-2 is our list of words, numbered both in decimal and binary. Note that capitalization counts: *an* and *An* are separate entries.

Table 6-2: Dictionary Compression

Position	Binary-encoded position	Word
1	00000	a
2	00001	an
3	00010	An
4	00011	animated
5	00100	animation
6	00101	are
7	00110	by
8	00111	called
9	01000	computer
10	01001	created
11	01010	entire
12	01011	from
13	01100	graphics
14	01101	in
15	01110	is
16	01111	movie
17	10000	of
18	10001	pictures
19	10010	sequence
20	10011	the
21	10100	these
22	10101	Those
23	10110	viewed
24	10111	When

As shown, 5 bits are sufficient to represent the range of positions used. Each word in the original paragraph is replaced with its position in this table. For example, instead of using eight ASCII codes (64 bits) for each appearance of the word *computer*, the 5-bit dictionary entry is used instead.

The dictionary itself takes up space, however, and must be included in the compressed document, so we save space only when a word appears more than once. In this example, the total number of letters for all words in our dictionary is 116, requiring 116 bytes. Replacing each of the 48 words in the sample paragraph with a 5-bit dictionary reference requires 235 bits, or about 30 bytes. The total compressed storage, then, is 146 bytes, which compared to the original 234 uncompressed bytes is a compression ratio of about 8:5. With longer documents the savings will be even better, because the text grows much faster than the dictionary. A typical novel, for example, is about 80,000 words long, but uses a vocabulary of only a few thousand words.

Huffman Encoding

In almost every text, some words are used much more than others. A technique called *Huffman encoding* takes advantage of this fact to improve on basic dictionary compression.

To create a Huffman code, the words in the document are ranked by frequency. Imagine a children's story with the 10-word vocabulary shown in Table 6-3. As with basic dictionary compression, each word is assigned a binary code, but here shorter codes are assigned to the words that appear most frequently in the story.

Table 6-3: Huffman Code for a Children's Story

Word	Frequency	Binary code
the	25%	01
a	20%	000
princess	12%	100
good	11%	110
witch	10%	111
evil	8%	0010
ate	7%	0011
magic	4%	1010
toadstool	2%	10110
forevermore	1%	10111

With the table in place, Huffman code compression is the same as basic dictionary compression: each word is replaced with its corresponding binary code. For example, the encoding for *the princess ate a magic toadstool* would start with 01 for *the*, then 100 for *princess*, and so on. In full, the encoding is:

011000011000101010110

As you may have noticed, the list of binary codes in Table 6-3 skips some possible codes, such as 011 or 0110. Skipping codes is necessary to make this a *prefix code*, in which no binary code appears at the start of another. For example, because 01 is the code for *the*, other codes that begin with 01, such as 011 or 0110, are forbidden. Because the individual codes vary in length, a prefix code is necessary to know where each code ends. With our example, the 01 that begins the bit sequence must be the code for *the* because no other code starts with 01; the only way to partition the whole sequence is as:

---

01 100 0011 000 1010 10110

If we allowed a code that broke the prefix rule, the sequences could become ambiguous. Suppose *forevermore* is assigned the code 00. While this is a shorter code, it means the example sequence could also be partitioned as:

---

01 100 00 110 00 1010 10110

This would decode as the phrase *the princess forevermore good forevermore magic toadstool*.

By assigning the shortest codes to the most common words, Huffman encoding can achieve greater compression than dictionary compression alone when data can be stored as a relatively small set of codes and some codes are more common than others.

Reorganizing Data for Better Compression

Unfortunately, the images we see in videos are not good candidates for Huffman encoding. Unlike the color-block images we compressed with the run-length technique, the pixels in a video image vary across the full range of possible colors. With 16 million different possible RGB colors, it's unlikely video images will have enough repetition to allow Huffman encoding to work. However, sometimes it's possible to create repetition in varied data by changing how the data is stored.

Predictive Encoding

For one such approach, consider a weather station that records the temperature once per hour, and over the course of one day stores the following readings:

51, 52, 53, 54, 55, 55, 56, 58, 60, 62, 65, 67, 68, 69, 71, 70, 68, 66, 63, 61, 59, 57, 54, 51

Dictionary compression and Huffman encoding are at the heart of most general compression schemes. The *.zip* archive format, for example, can choose from a half-dozen compression methods but usually employs an algorithm called *deflate*. Rather than replacing duplicated data with a reference number from a list of words, this algorithm employs a variation of dictionary compression called a *sliding window*.

With this method, duplicate data is replaced with numerical indicators showing where the data occurred previously. In the textual example of Figure 6-2, there are three duplicate runs of characters. The first member of each pair is the number of characters to go back, and the second number is the length of the run. For example, the pair 5, 2 means "go back five characters, and copy two characters."

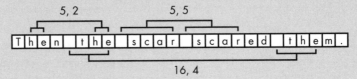

Figure 6-2: Sliding-window compression

The compressed version of this text can be symbolically written as "Then t[5,2] scar[5,5]ed[16,4]m." Instead of the number pairs being stored directly, though, they are Huffman-encoded, so the most commonly occurring pairs are assigned shorter codes. The deflate method is a highly effective general compression scheme, capable of reducing the 3,138,473 characters in a raw text version of Tolstoy's *War and Peace* to a *.zip* file of around 930,000 bytes, about a 10:3 ratio.

If we assume a temperature range of 120 to −50, we can store each temperature in an 8-bit byte, using 192 bits total. There aren't many duplicates in this list, though, so Huffman encoding won't be effective. The situation improves if we rewrite this list using *predictive encoding*. For every temperature after the first, we'll record not the temperature itself, but its difference from the previous temperature. Now the list looks like this:

(51): 1, 1, 1, 1, 0, 1, 2, 2, 2, 3, 2, 1, 1, 2, -1, -2, -2, -3, -2, -2, -2, -3, -3

Whereas the original data had few duplicates, the predictive-encoded data has many. Now we can apply Huffman encoding with excellent results.

Quantization

Another approach, if we are willing to accept some degradation of the data, is *quantization*, where we store the data with less precision. Suppose the weather station from the previous example also records daily rainfall amounts, taking the following readings over the course of three weeks:

0.01, 1.23, 1.21, 0.02, 0.01, 0.87, 0.57, 0.60, 0.02, 0.00, 0.03, 0.03, 2.45, 2.41, 0.82, 0.53, 1.29, 0.02, 0.01, 0.01, 0.04

These readings have two decimal places, but maybe we don't actually need this much precision in the data. For one thing, any amount below 0.05 might represent condensation on the collector rather than actual rain; likewise, condensation might also be the only difference between readings like 1.23 and 1.21. So let's leave off the last digit of every number:

0.0, 1.2, 1.2, 0.0, 0.0, 0.8, 0.5, 0.6, 0.0, 0.0, 0.0, 0.0, 2.4, 2.4, 0.8, 0.5, 1.2, 0.0, 0.0, 0.0, 0.0

By itself, this compresses the data, since storing one place after the decimal will take fewer bits than storing two. In addition, the quantized data also has several runs of zeros that can be compressed with run-length encoding, and some duplicates that can be compressed by Huffman encoding.

These techniques point to a general multistage approach for compression. First, reorganize the data to increase the runs and duplicates, by storing small differences between numbers rather than the raw numbers themselves, quantizing the data, or both. Then compress the data with run-length and Huffman encoding.

JPEG Images

We now have almost all the tools needed to compress video. The logical first step in compressing a video is to compress the individual images in the video. However, we can't directly apply predictive encoding and quantization to digital photographs and other images with lots of subtle color variation; we need to convert these pictures to another format first.

That's the idea behind *JPEG*, a common compressed-image format designed specifically for digital photographs. (The name is the acronym for the *Joint Photography Experts Group* that developed the format.) The compression method for this format is based on a couple of key observations of photography and human perception.

First, although pixel colors may vary widely throughout an image, individual pixels tend to be similar to their neighbors. If you take a picture of a leafy tree against a partly cloudy sky, lots of green leaf pixels will be next to other green pixels, blue sky pixels will neighbor blue sky pixels, and gray cloud pixels will neighbor gray cloud pixels.

Second, among neighboring pixels, there will be more noticeable variation in brightness levels than in color tone. For our tree photograph, each of the myriad leaf pixels will reflect a different quantity of sunlight, but the underlying color of each pixel will be roughly similar. Also, although the mechanisms of human vision are not completely understood, tests indicate that we perceive differences in brightness more distinctly than differences in color.

High compression of digital photographs is possible only with lossy compression; we have to accept some degradation of the image. Following these key observations, though, allows the JPEG format to throw away the data that is least likely to be missed. In our tree photograph, the most important distinctions are the broad differences between leaf and sky, or sky and cloud, not between two neighboring cloud pixels. After that, the most important distinction is the relative brightness of pixels, more so than relative color. The JPEG format therefore gives priority to broad differences over fine differences, and brightness over color.

A Different Way to Store Colors

JPEG compression divides images into 8×8 blocks of pixels that are independently compressed. To compress brightness and color differently, each pixel's R, G, and B values are converted to three other numbers Y, Cb, and Cr. Here, Y is the *luminance* of the pixel, or how much light the pixel produces. Cb is the *blue difference*, and Cr is the *red difference*. The simplest way to envision the YCbCr system is to imagine a dark green video screen with three knobs labeled Y, Cb, and Cr initially set to zero: turn up Y and the screen is brighter; turn up Cb and the screen becomes more blue and less green; turn up Cr and the screen becomes more red and less green. Table 6-4 lists a few named colors in both systems for comparison. (A historical note: YCbCr is derived from the color system used in broadcast television. In the early days of color television, the remaining black-and-white televisions could properly display color transmissions by interpreting only the Y component of the signal.)

Table 6-4: Select Colors in the RGB and YCbCr Color Systems

R	G	B	Color description	Y	Cb	Cr
0	255	0	Lime green	145	54	34
255	255	255	Pure white	235	128	128
0	255	255	Aqua	170	166	16
128	0	0	Maroon	49	109	184

JPEG compresses the Y, Cb, and Cr data separately, so we can think of each 8×8 block of pixels as becoming three 8×8 blocks of Y, Cb, and Cr data. Separating the data this way takes advantage of the greater variation in brightness than in color. Under the YCbCr system, most of the differences between the pixels will be concentrated in the Y component. The lower variance in the Cb and Cr blocks will make them easier to compress, and because we're more sensitive to variations in luminance than variations of color, the Cb and Cr blocks can be compressed more heavily.

The Discrete Cosine Transform

The conversion to YCbCr follows the observation that brightness is more important than color. To take advantage of the greater importance of broad changes over narrow changes, though, we need to convert each 8×8 data blocks yet again. The *discrete cosine transform (DCT)* converts the absolute luminance and color data into relative measurements of how these values differ from pixel to pixel. Although this transformation is applied to an entire 8×8 block of numbers, I'll first illustrate the idea with a single row of eight numbers from the luminance (Y) block, shown as shades of gray in Figure 6-3.

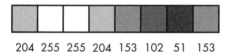

204 255 255 204 153 102 51 153

Figure 6-3: A row of luminance levels

To begin the DCT, we subtract 128 from each number, which has the effect of moving the 0–255 range to a range centered around 0, so that maximum brightness is 127 and absolute black is −128. The resulting luminance levels for the row are depicted as a line chart in Figure 6-4.

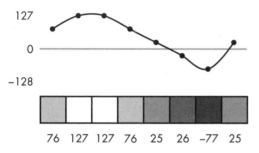

76 127 127 76 25 26 −77 25

Figure 6-4: Subtracting 128 from each luminance level centers the range of possible numbers around 0.

The DCT produces eight new numbers that each combine the eight luminance levels in a different way. Figure 6-5 shows the DCT of the previous figure.

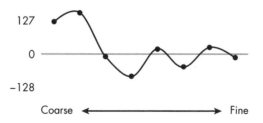

Coarse ⟵⟶ Fine

Figure 6-5: The discrete cosine transform of the data in Figure 6-4.

Note that the numbers are labeled with a range from "coarse" to "fine." The leftmost number in the DCT is the simplest combination of the luminance levels: their sum. Thus, the first number is the overall brightness of the pixels, and will be positive for a bright row of pixels and negative for a dark row. The second number effectively compares the luminance levels on the left end of the row against those on the right, and is positive in this example because our luminance levels are brighter on the left than on the right. The rightmost number effectively compares each luminance value against its immediate neighbors, and is close to 0 here because the numbers in Figure 6-4 change gradually.

These DCT numbers are the coefficients that result from an operation called *matrix multiplication*. If your eyes just glazed over, don't worry: the operation involves nothing more than multiplication and addition. We produce each coefficient by multiplying the luminance values by a different, predetermined vector. In this context, a *vector* is just an ordered list of numbers. The eight vectors used in the DCT are illustrated in Figure 6-6. (The numbers in each vector are related to the cosine function from trigonometry, which is where the discrete cosine transform gets its name, but we can safely ignore that for this discussion.)

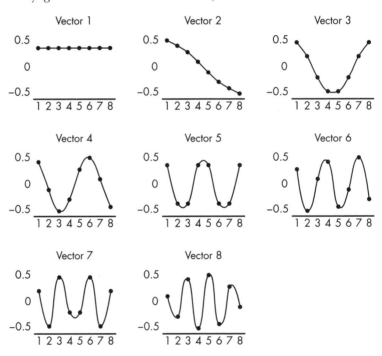

Figure 6-6: The vectors needed for our single-row DCT

To produce a coefficient for our luminance row, we multiply each number in a vector by the luminance in the same position. For example, Table 6-5 shows the computation of the Vector 2 coefficient for our luminance row. Each number from the luminance row is multiplied by the number in the same position in Vector 1; then, these products are summed to get 157.386.

Table 6-5: Computing the Coefficient for Vector 2

Position	Luminance (from Figure 6-4)	Vector	Product
1	76	0.49	37.24
2	127	0.416	52.832
3	127	0.278	35.306
4	76	0.098	7.448
5	25	−0.098	−2.45
6	−26	−0.278	7.228
7	−77	−0.416	32.032
8	25	−0.49	−12.25
Total			157.386

Looking at the vectors of Figure 6-6, you can see how each combines the luminance levels differently. Because every number in Vector 1 is the same positive number, the Vector 1 coefficient becomes a measure of overall brightness. Because Vector 2's numbers gradually sweep from high to low, the second coefficient will be positive when luminance tends to fall off from the left to right in the pixel row, and negative when luminance tends to increase. Vector 3's coefficient is a measure of how the ends of the row differ from the middle, and so on. You've already seen the resulting coefficients charted in Figure 6-5; Table 6-6 shows the result numerically.

Table 6-6: Coefficients from the Discrete Cosine Transform of the Sample Luminance Row

Vector number	Coefficient
1	124.804
2	157.296
3	−9.758
4	−87.894
5	18.031
6	−49.746
7	23.559
8	−13.096

The process is reversible: we can retrieve the original luminance numbers from Figure 6-4 by multiplying the eight coefficients against eight different vectors, a process called the *inverse discrete cosine transform (IDCT)*. Table 6-7 shows how the second luminance value, 127, is extracted from the coefficients.

Table 6-7: Computing the Second Luminance Value from the Coefficients

Position	Coefficient	Vector	Product
1	124.804	0.354	44.125
2	157.296	0.416	65.393
3	–9.758	0.191	–1.867
4	–87.894	–0.098	8.574
5	18.031	–0.354	–6.375
6	–49.746	–0.49	24.395
7	–23.559	–0.462	–10.833
8	–13.096	–0.278	3.638
Total			127

The DCT, then, gives us a different way of storing the same numbers: as the relationship between the data rather than the data itself. Why is this useful? Remember that fine distinctions between pixels are less noticeable than broader distinctions. Later, you'll see how the DCT allows the JPEG format to compress the fine details more than the broad.

The DCT for Two Dimensions

JPEG compression works not on rows of pixels but on 8×8 pixel blocks, so now let's see how the DCT operates in two dimensions. The one-dimensional DCT multiplies eight vectors with the original eight numbers to produce eight coefficients. The two-dimensional DCT, though, requires 64 *matrices*, each matrix being an 8×8 table of numbers. Like the vectors, each matrix will multiply all 64 pieces of data in the 8×8 block.

The matrices themselves are two-dimensional combinations of the vectors we saw earlier. This is easiest to understand pictorially. Figure 6-7 shows the combination of a horizontal Vector 1 and a vertical Vector 1. Because the numbers in Vector 1 are all the same, the numbers in the resulting matrix are as well. In these matrix illustrations, lighter gray means a higher number.

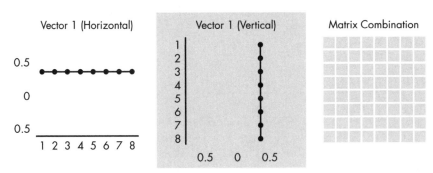

Figure 6-7: The matrix combination of Vector 1 and itself

In Figure 6-8, horizontal Vector 1 is combined with vertical Vector 2. The resulting matrix gradually varies from top to bottom as Vector 2 gradually varies, but doesn't vary left to right because the numbers in Vector 1 don't vary.

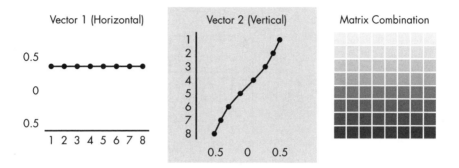

Figure 6-8: The matrix combination of Vector 1 and Vector 2

Figure 6-9 shows a last example, Vector 8 combined with Vector 8. Because Vector 8 swings back and forth from positive to negative, the combination matrix has a checkerboard quality.

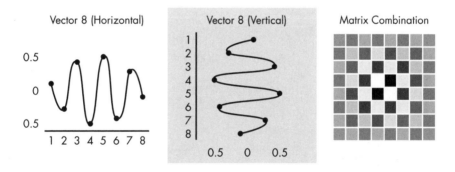

Figure 6-9: The matrix combination of Vector 8 and itself

The two-dimensional DCT replaces each of the 64 numbers in an 8×8 block with a matrix coefficient. Figure 6-10 shows which matrices are used for a few locations. Similar to the one-dimensional DCT, the coefficient in the upper left, which is the same shown in Figure 6-7, sums all the numbers in the original block equally. As we progress downward and to the right, the distinctions being measured grow finer.

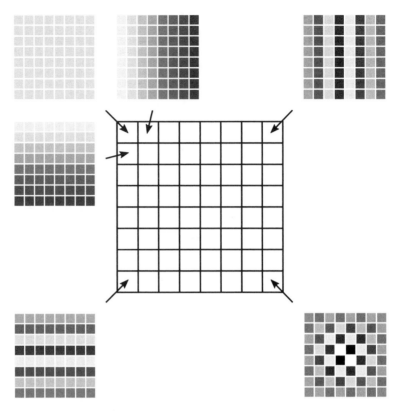

Figure 6-10: Some of the matrices used in the two-dimensional DCT

To demonstrate the two-dimensional DCT, I'll use just the luminance values of the pixel block shown in Figure 6-11.

8×8 Block of Pixels   Luminance (Y) Values

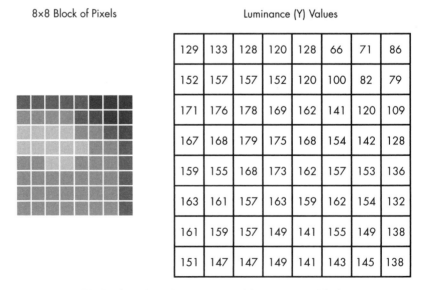

129	133	128	120	128	66	71	86
152	157	157	152	120	100	82	79
171	176	178	169	162	141	120	109
167	168	179	175	168	154	142	128
159	155	168	173	162	157	153	136
163	161	157	163	159	162	154	132
161	159	157	149	141	155	149	138
151	147	147	149	141	143	145	138

Figure 6-11: A block of pixels and the associated luminance (Y) block

Figure 6-12 shows the same luminance block with 128 subtracted from each number to make a range from −127 to 128 centered around 0.

1	5	0	−8	0	−62	−57	−42
24	29	29	24	−8	−28	−46	−49
43	48	50	41	34	13	−8	−19
39	40	51	47	40	26	14	0
31	27	40	45	34	29	25	8
35	33	29	35	31	34	26	4
33	31	29	21	13	27	21	10
23	19	19	21	13	15	17	10

Figure 6-12: The luminance block from Figure 6-11 with the range of possible values centered around 0

Figure 6-13 shows the luminance block after DCT. Each number is the coefficient resulting from multiplying the matrix of luminance values in Figure 6-12 with one of the matrices from Figure 6-10. Remember that these numbers, too, are centered around 0. So the 132 in the upper left, for example, indicates a high luminance level for the block as a whole. Notice that the numbers in the upper left are largest in magnitude (furthest from 0 in either direction), indicating that broad luminance differences are much greater than the fine differences in this pixel block. This result is typical of JPEG-encoded photographs.

132	110	−43	−3	1	5	−3	−3
−85	71	−22	−20	19	−15	−5	10
−103	13	20	−12	11	−10	−5	3
−34	−13	6	2	7	−2	−6	4
−15	−21	−1	−7	12	−2	−4	10
9	−5	6	3	0	−9	0	8
9	−6	−4	7	5	−7	−6	6
3	−5	2	−1	1	−2	1	3

Figure 6-13: The DCT of the block in Figure 6-12

Compressing the Results

Now the real compression can begin, the first step of which is quantization. Figure 6-14 shows the 8×8 block of divisors used for quantizing the luminance block. Each number in the coefficient block of Figure 6-13 is divided by the number in the same position in Figure 6-14, with results rounded to the nearest whole number. This degrades the image through quantization error, but note that the divisors in Figure 6-14 are smallest in the upper left. Thus, the quantization error is most pronounced in the coefficients that measure the finest distinctions, where the error is least likely to be noticed. The actual values of the divisors varies according to the compression quality, with larger divisors used to quantize the Cr and Cb blocks, but the divisor block always follows this general pattern (lower values in the upper left, higher in the bottom right).

16	11	10	16	25	40	51	61
12	12	14	19	26	58	60	55
14	13	16	24	40	57	69	59
14	17	22	29	51	87	80	62
18	22	37	56	68	109	103	77
24	35	55	64	81	104	113	92
49	64	78	87	103	121	120	101
72	92	95	98	112	100	103	99

Figure 6-14: The divisors used to quantize luminance blocks

The result of quantization for our sample block is shown in Figure 6-15.

You can see how suitable these numbers are for run-length and Huffman encoding. Most of the coefficients have been quantized all the way down to 0, with many duplicate coefficients among the rest.

After quantization, nonzero results tend to cluster in the upper left of the matrix, so the quantized numbers are listed in the zigzag pattern shown in Figure 6-16.

8	10	-4	0	0	0	0	0
-7	6	-2	-1	1	0	0	0
-7	1	1	0	0	0	0	0
-2	-1	0	0	0	0	0	0
-1	-1	0	0	0	0	0	0
0	0	0	0	0	0	0	0
0	0	0	0	0	0	0	0
0	0	0	0	0	0	0	0

Figure 6-15: The quantized luminance block

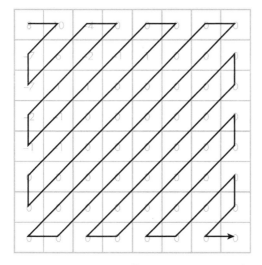

Figure 6-16: Storing coefficients in a zigzag order

This zigzag pattern tends to produce a very long run of zeros at the end, as it does in our example:

8 10 -7 -7 6 -4 0 -2 1 -2 -1 -1 1 -1 0 0 1 0 0 -1 0 0 0 0 0 0 0 0 0 0 0 0
0 0 0 0 0 0 0 0 0 0 0 0 0 0 0 0 0 0 0 0 0 0 0 0 0 0 0 0 0 0 0 0

To encode the runs of zeros, we replace each nonzero entry in the list by a pair of numbers: the number of zeros skipped (possibly none), and the coefficient itself. For example, the eighth number in our list is a –2 that is preceded by one 0. This would become the number pair 1, –2. At this stage, our list looks like this:

```
0, 8
0, 10
0, -7
0, -7
0, 6
0, -4
1, -2
0, 1
0, -2
0, -1
0, -1
0, 1
0, -1
1, -1
2, 1
2, -1
(all the rest are zero)
```

Some of these number pairs, such as 0, –1, appear very frequently in these lists compared to other pairs like 0, 10. For maximum compression, the JPEG standard defines a Huffman encoding for every possible number pair in these lists. The common 0, –1 pair, for example, becomes the short Huffman code 001, while the uncommon 0, 10 pair becomes the longer code 10110010. There's also a special code, 1010, to signal that all the rest of the coefficients in the list are 0. The Huffman encoding for our list is shown in Table 6-8.

Table 6-8: The Huffman Encoding of the Coefficients from Figure 6-15

Zeros skipped	Coefficient	Huffman encoding
0	8	10110000
0	10	10110010
0	–7	100111
0	–7	100111
0	6	100010
0	–4	100100
1	–2	11100110
0	1	000
0	–2	0110
0	–1	001
0	–1	001
0	1	000
0	–1	001

Zeros skipped	Coefficient	Huffman encoding
1	−1	11001
2	1	110110
2	−1	110111
(Nothing left but zeros)		1010

All of the bits in the rightmost column, strung together, represent the compressed encoding of our original luminance block. The original block represented the luminance levels as 64 bytes, or 512 bits total. In contrast, the encoding in Table 6-8 uses a mere 88 bits.

The two color blocks, Cr and Cb, would show even higher compression because the divisors used on the color blocks are even larger, which produces smaller numbers with shorter Huffman codes and more zeros for the run-length encoding. Overall, JPEG images typically achieve a 10:1 compression ratio. The amount of compression can be increased or reduced by using smaller or larger divisors than those shown in Figure 6-14. These divisors are adjusted by the "quality" slider in image-manipulation programs. Sliding the control to "low quality" increases the divisors, reducing the file size while increasing the quantization error.

JPEG Picture Quality

High compression is great only if the restored image is indistinguishable from the original, or nearly so. Typically the alterations JPEG compression makes to an image are difficult to see. To get a feel for the changes introduced by compression, let's compare the original block of luminance values to the block that results from compressing and decompressing, as shown in Figure 6-17.

Original Luminance Block

129	133	128	120	128	66	71	86
152	157	157	152	120	100	82	79
171	176	178	169	162	141	120	109
167	168	179	175	168	154	142	128
159	155	168	173	162	157	153	136
163	161	157	163	159	162	154	132
161	159	157	149	141	155	149	138
151	147	147	149	141	143	145	138

Reconstructed Luminance Block

130	127	129	130	112	84	71	74
158	154	155	153	132	102	86	85
174	173	174	172	155	129	111	107
165	168	173	174	166	150	137	130
156	161	165	166	165	160	150	141
159	163	162	158	158	159	151	139
159	161	156	146	147	154	148	136
151	153	145	135	138	150	147	135

Figure 6-17: The original luminance block, and the result of compressing and decompressing the block

Since it's tough to visually compare these two blocks of numbers, Figure 6-18 shows the differences as a grayscale matrix. As you can see, most of the matrix is neutral gray, indicating numbers very close to the original.

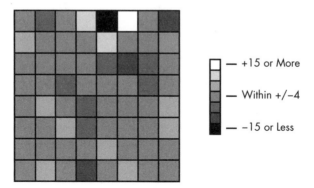

Figure 6-19: The amount of error in each location of the luminance block

The best evidence for the quality of JPEGs is shown in Figure 6-19. On the top is an uncompressed digital photograph. Because this photo is in grayscale, we don't need RGB pixel color, just a single byte indicating the grayscale level. At a resolution of 975×731, this uncompressed photo requires just under 713 kilobytes of storage. In the middle is a compressed JPEG version of the original photo, requiring just 75 kilobytes of storage, which is virtually indistinguishable from the original. The photo on the bottom is a low-quality JPEG using larger divisors. While the photo takes up only about 7 kilobytes, compression artifacts are clearly visible. Many of the individual 8×8 pixel blocks have been reduced to solid squares of the same gray level. In general, JPEG can result in a 10:1 compression ratio without sacrificing visual quality.

Compressing High-Definition Video

The JPEG format does a fantastic job of compressing images with only small sacrifices in quality, but for high-definition video we need even more compression. Remember, uncompressed high-definition video requires about 186MBps. Individually compressing each image as a JPEG would reduce that requirement to about 18MBps—a big improvement, but for streaming or disc storage we need to shrink the data to just a few MBps per second.

Figure 6-18: An uncompressed photo (top), high-quality JPEG compression (middle), and low-quality JPEG compression (bottom)

Temporal Redundancy

To hit this target, video compression techniques take advantage of similarities between images in sequence. Figure 6-20 shows an image sequence from a movie's opening credits.

Figure 6-20: A few frames of an opening title sequence

Each of these images will be shown for several seconds; which means that the sequence will contain many duplicate frames in a row. Also, even as the video transitions from one image to the next, most of the picture remains unchanged. Only the area in the center varies.

Now consider the image sequence shown in Figure 6-21. Although each frame differs from the next, the same elements are present in each frame, just in different places on the screen.

Figure 6-21: An image sequence with a moving object

These examples show two different forms of *temporal redundancy*, continuity of data from one frame to the next. Compression that exploits such redundancy is called *temporal compression*, and as we'll see in the next section, it's the key to achieving the compression ratios needed for video streaming and storage.

MPEG-2 Video Compression

One method of temporal compression is employed by *MPEG-2*, a common video format supported by Blu-ray discs and digital broadcast television. More advanced techniques exist, but they are extensions of the ideas demonstrated here.

Groups of Frames

MPEG-2 videos are divided into sequences of around 15 frames called *groups of pictures (GOPs)*. Exactly one frame in each GOP is selected to be a basic JPEG-encoded image called an *intracoded frame (I-Frame)*. This frame is the rock upon which the rest of the GOP is built. All of the other frames use temporal compression, which means they are stored not as the absolute colors of the pixels in the image, but by how those colors differ from those in another image in the GOP, as we'll see shortly.

The other frames in the group are assigned one of two types, *predicted frames (P-Frames)* and *bidirectional frames (B-Frames)*. A P-Frame stores the difference between its pixels and those of a previous frame, while a B-Frame stores the difference between its pixels and those of a previous *and* a later frame.

A GOP is shown in Figure 6-22, with arrows indicating the frames referenced by the temporal compression. As you can see, everything depends on the I-Frame. During playback, it must be decoded before any other image in the GOP, after which the frames that directly reference the I-Frame can be decoded, and so on.

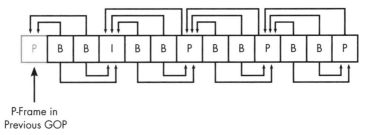

P-Frame in
Previous GOP

Figure 6-22: A GOP, or group of pictures

Grouping pictures this way simplifies encoding and decoding, and also limits the length of the reference "chain." Just like a photocopy of a photocopy, the longer the chain of temporal compression, the fuzzier the image gets. The regular appearance of I-Frames is also what allows you to see images as you fast-forward or rewind; the video player just picks out the I-Frames, which can be decoded and displayed independently of the other frames in its GOP.

The MPEG specification gives encoding software wide discretion in forming GOPs. The number of I-Frames, which directly determines the size of GOPs, is up to the encoder, as is the number of B-Frames between the other frame types. Like the divisors used in JPEG quantization, the ability to change the relative numbers of the three frame types offers a trade-off between quality and compression. In applications where compression is paramount, like videoconferencing, I-Frames are rare and B-Frames are common, while in a Blu-ray, the encoder will use as many I-Frames as possible while still fitting all the video data on the disc.

Temporal Compression

So how does the temporal compression of P-Frames and B-Frames work? In this example, we're compressing a P-Frame by referencing an I-Frame. First, the pixels in the P-Frame are divided into 16×16 *macroblocks*. For each macroblock, the I-Frame is searched for a matching block of pixels with the same color data. This matching block may not appear in exactly the same place in the I-Frame, though, so it is indicated by its *offset*: the difference between the location in the P-Frame and the location in the I-Frame, expressed in screen coordinates. For example, an offset of −100, 50 indicates that the macroblock's location in the I-Frame is 100 pixels left and 50 pixels down from its location in the P-Frame, as shown in Figure 6-23.

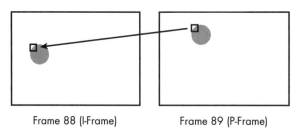

Frame 88 (I-Frame)   Frame 89 (P-Frame)

Figure 6-23: A macroblock in a P-Frame referencing a matching block of pixels in a previous frame

In most cases, an exact match won't be found, so in addition to storing the location of the best match, the differences between the two macroblocks must also be stored. Figure 6-24 shows a luminance block from the P-Frame and the best match in the I-Frame. (I'm using 8×8 blocks instead of a full 16×16 macroblock to keep the example manageable.)

Luminance Block from P-Frame

129	111	125	116	147	66	99	86
155	157	165	150	123	100	88	79
171	188	178	166	166	146	75	111
167	168	175	175	174	159	142	130
159	158	164	171	173	157	160	136
175	168	150	160	160	157	163	130
172	164	157	149	142	150	143	138
151	144	147	149	145	143	142	150

Luminance Block from I-Frame

129	133	128	120	128	66	71	86
152	157	157	152	120	100	82	79
171	176	178	169	162	141	120	109
167	168	179	175	168	154	142	128
159	155	168	173	162	157	153	136
163	161	157	163	159	162	154	132
161	159	157	149	141	155	149	138
151	147	147	149	141	143	145	138

Figure 6-24: A luminance block and its best match in a prior frame

Next, a block of differences is computed: each number in the I-Frame block is subtracted from the number in the same position in the P-Frame block. The result for our example is shown in Figure 6-25.

Luminance Difference

0	22	3	4	-19	0	-28	0
-3	0	-8	2	-3	0	-6	0
0	-12	0	3	-4	-5	45	-2
0	0	4	0	-6	-5	0	-2
0	-3	4	2	-11	0	-7	0
-12	-7	7	3	-1	5	-9	2
-11	-5	0	0	-1	5	6	0
0	3	0	0	-4	0	3	-12

Figure 6-25: The difference between the two luminance blocks in Figure 6-24

Because the blocks are a close match, these values are all small. This is a form of predictive encoding, just like the list of temperatures shown earlier in the chapter. By storing differences, we've made the range of data much smaller, and therefore more easily compressed. When we apply the DCT and quantize the results, the numbers are downright tiny, as shown in Figure 6-26.

Luminance Difference after DCT

0	0	0	-1	0	0	0	0
0	1	1	0	0	0	0	0
0	1	0	0	0	0	0	0
-1	1	0	0	0	0	0	0
0	1	0	0	0	0	0	0
0	0	0	0	0	0	0	0
0	0	0	0	0	0	0	0
0	0	0	0	0	0	0	0

Figure 6-26: The result of quantizing the block in Figure 6-25 and applying the DCT

This block is highly susceptible to the last stage of compression: the combination of run-length and Huffman encoding. As shown in Table 6-9, the original luminance block has been reduced to a mere 39 bits.

Table 6-9: The Huffman Encoding of the Numbers in Figure 6-26

Run length	Coefficient	Huffman encoding
4	1	1110110
1	–1	11001
0	1	000
0	1	000
0	–1	001
1	1	11000
7	1	111110100
(Nothing left but zeros)		1010

Not every macroblock in the P-Frame is encoded in this way. In some cases, a macroblock may not be similar enough to any block of pixels in the previous frame to save any space by storing the difference. Those macroblocks can be recorded directly, like the macroblocks in an I-Frame. For a B-Frame, matching macroblocks can be found in a previous frame or a later frame, which improves the odds of a close match.

Video Quality with Temporal Compression

Temporal compression depends upon temporal redundancy—sequences of frames with few changes. For this reason, some videos compress much better than others. Movies with lots of camera movement, like *Cloverfield* or *The Blair Witch Project*, are difficult to compress, while movies with long takes where the camera doesn't move, like *2001: A Space Odyssey*, are ideal.

Ultimately, video compression is a bit of an art as well as a science. As stated earlier, different MPEG-2 encoders can produce different results for the same sequence of images. Shorter GOPs, with more I-Frames and fewer B-Frames, produce better-looking video than longer GOPs, but longer GOPs mean better compression. An encoder can vary the mix of frames even within the same video, using longer GOPs when there's high temporal redundancy and shorter GOPs when there isn't. Also, good encoders will try to line up GOP boundaries with sharp cuts in a movie; if you've ever seen a video that was momentarily very blocky when the scene changed, it's likely because a GOP stretched over the cut.

There's also the question of performance, especially if the video is being compressed in real time, as with a live event. There might not be enough time to find the absolute best match for a macroblock in the other frame.

Playback quality can vary as well. For example, because of how frames are broken into individually processed macroblocks, seams may appear along the borders of the blocks. To reduce this effect, a decoder may apply a *deblocking filter*. This smoothes block boundaries by averaging pixel colors, much like the anti-aliasing methods shown in previous chapters. The strength of the filter can be adjusted based on the likelihood of a clean boundary. In a B-Frame, for example, if one block references the previous frame while an adjacent block references the next frame, there's a greater likelihood of a rough boundary, which calls for stronger filtering.

In other cases, the resolution of the video and the display resolution may not match. For example, when you're streaming an episode of the old cop show *Adam-12* (it's not just me, right?) on a high-definition television, either the television or the player has to convert the original 640×480 images to fill the 1920×1080 display. This is the same problem we solved in Chapter 5 with texture mapping—applying a bitmap to a larger area—and video devices can employ the same sorts of techniques. Early high-definition players effectively used nearest-neighbor sampling, which produced poor results. Newer players employ techniques similar to trilinear filtering. Instead of blending between bilinear samples from two different levels in a mipmap, however, they blend between successive frames. This is especially effective in smoothing objects in motion.

Although not as computationally intense as the original encoding, playing back a temporally compressed video is still a lot of work for a processor. Also, the structure of a GOP requires decoding the frames out of order. This in turn requires that frames be *buffered*, held in a queue prior to display. For streaming video, much larger buffers are used so that minor hiccups in the network don't disrupt playback.

The Present and Future of Video Compression

The latest video compression standard, known as H.264 or MPEG-4, extends the techniques used in MPEG-2 but isn't fundamentally different. The primary differences improve the quality of macroblock matching. Instead of being matched against just one or two other frames, macroblocks can be matched against 32 other frames. Also, the 16×16 macroblocks themselves can be broken down into separately matched 8×8 blocks.

Through such improvements, MPEG-4 can often achieve twice the compression ratio of MPEG-2 with the same quality result. For that reason, MPEG-4 is an industry standard for both streaming and storage. Most Blu-ray videos use it, as do YouTube and Netflix. Its chief competition is a format called Theora, which uses similar compression methods but is freely licensed, unlike the proprietary MPEG-4.

Today's compression formats do an amazing job at shrinking video data, but they do so at a high computational cost. The next time you watch a clip on YouTube, think about a GOP, all the macroblocks being copied and updated from one frame to the next, and all the number crunching that goes into performing the DCT over and over again. It's a dizzying amount of calculation just to show a cat falling off a piano.

Even more computational horsepower will be needed in the future. The new *ultra high definition (UHD)* format, seen in theaters in films like Peter Jackson's *Hobbit* series, is starting to trickle down to home video. UHD images are 3840×2160, which is four times the number of pixels as current high definition. The frame rate will also increase, from today's 24 or 30 fps to 48, 60, or even 120 fps. UHD video could increase the bit requirements from today's 1,400Mbps to over 23,000, which will require a corresponding increase in bandwidth and disc storage capacity—unless someone clever comes up with an even better way for software to shrink the data.

7

SEARCH

This chapter is about a topic that, perhaps more than any other subject covered in this book, we all take for granted: finding the data we want, known as a *search*. Searching happens so often, and so quickly, that it's easy to miss the magic. When a word processor underlines a misspelled word that you just typed, a fast search has taken place behind the scenes. When you enter part of a filename and get a list of matching files on your laptop's hard drive, that's another near-instant search. And then there's the ultimate search achievement: the Web. The Web is so unfathomably large that we can only guess its true size, and yet, web search engines can find relevant web pages in a fraction of a second.

How does software find what we want so fast?

Defining the Search Problem

Let's start by getting our terminology straight. A collection of data is known, appropriately enough, as a *data collection*. Each item in the data collection is a *record*. A record is uniquely identified by a *key* (no relation to the cryptography term). A search retrieves the record that matches a given key. For a real-world example, when you use a dictionary the word you're looking up is the key, and the definition of that word is the record.

The main goal of searching is to find the right record. But the speed of the search is just as important. If searches could go on indefinitely, searching would be simple. But as the wait time increases, so does our frustration. The length of time we'll wait on a search varies, but it's never very long, and in many situations, the search must appear to finish instantaneously.

Putting Data in Order

Efficient searching requires well-organized data. When you visit a bookstore, for example, finding a novel by a particular author is easy if the store has ordered the shelves by authors' last names. For one thing, you know where to start looking. Once you look at the first book on the shelf and see how close its author's name is alphabetically to the author you seek, you would have a good idea where to look next.

If the store didn't shelve its books in any particular order, then finding a book would be hard work. The best option is to start at one end of the shelf and examine every single book, which is known as a *sequential search*. In the worst case, the book you want isn't even on the shelf, but you wouldn't know that until you've looked through the whole collection.

Therefore, putting the data collection in a particular order, known as *sorting*, is essential for efficient searching. There are many different ways to sort; entire books have been written to describe different sorting algorithms for software. We'll look at two methods here.

Selection Sort

If I asked you to put a list of numbers in order, you would most likely use what is known as a *selection sort*. First, you'd scan the list to find the lowest number, and then you'd cross the number out and copy it to a new list. You would repeat the process until all the numbers were in order in the new, sorted list.

The first three steps of a selection sort of nine numbers are shown in Figure 7-1. In the first step, the lowest number is copied to the beginning of a new list. In the steps that follow, the lowest remaining numbers are copied to the new list.

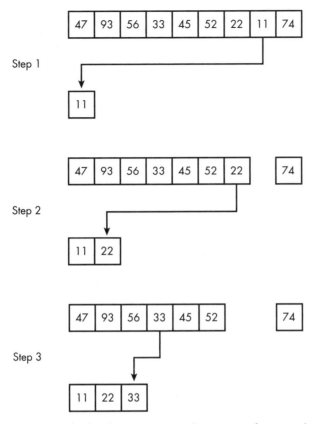

Figure 7-1: The first three steps in a selection sort of nine numbers

Quicksort

While selection sort is easy to understand, software rarely uses it because it isn't efficient. Each step requires us to process every number in the unsorted list, and for that effort all we get is one number in its correct position.

A better sorting method, called *quicksort*, partially orders all of the data processed during each pass, reducing later effort and time. Instead of scanning the entire list for the lowest number, we select a number in the list to be the *pivot*. We use the pivot to *partition* the list, dividing the list around the pivot. Numbers that are less than the pivot go to the front of the list, and those that are greater go to the back.

For this example we'll use the same list of numbers used in the selection sort. Figure 7-2 shows the first step of partitioning. Different versions of quicksort select the pivot in different way; we'll keep things simple and use the first number in the list, 47, as the pivot. The next number, 93, is copied to the end of the new list because it is greater than 47.

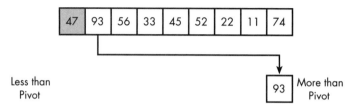

Figure 7-2: The number 93 is more than the pivot, so it moves to the end of the new list.

In Figure 7-3, 56 is also greater than 47, so it's copied to the next space on the end.

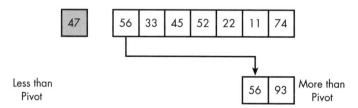

Figure 7-3: The number 56 is more than the pivot, so it moves to the end of the new list.

In Figure 7-4, 33 is less than 47, so it's copied to the front of the new list.

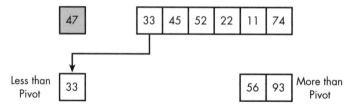

Figure 7-4: The number 33 is less than the pivot, so it moves to the front of the new list.

Figure 7-5 combines the next five steps. Three of the remaining numbers go to the front of the list and two go to the back. This leaves a gap for one more number.

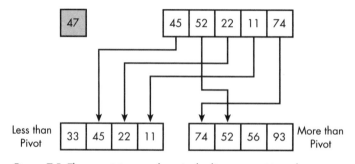

Figure 7-5: The remaining numbers in the list are partitioned.

In Figure 7-6, this gap is filled with 47, the pivot. This completes the initial partitioning.

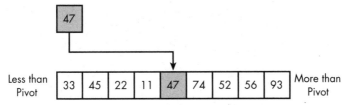

Figure 7-6: The pivot fills the open space in the new list.

This new list isn't sorted, but it's in better shape than before. The pivot is in its correct sorted position, indicated by the shading. The first four numbers in the list are less than 47, and the last four are greater than 47. A single partitioning does more than put one number in its correct place, like one step of a selection sort; it also divides the remaining numbers in the list into sublists, as shown in Figure 7-7. These sublists can be sorted independently. Sorting two shorter lists requires less effort than sorting one longer list. If you doubt this, consider an extreme case: would you rather sort 50 short lists of 2 numbers, or 1 long list of 100 numbers?

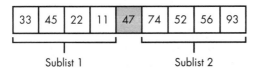

Figure 7-7: Partitioning has transformed the list into two separate, smaller lists that can be sorted independently.

The two sublists are now independently partitioned. In Figure 7-8, the first number in the sublist, 33, becomes the new pivot and the four numbers of sublist 1 are partitioned. This puts 22 and 11 to the left of the 33, and 45 to the right.

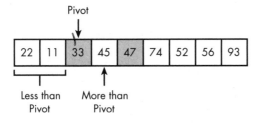

Figure 7-8: Partitioning sublist 1 of Figure 7-7

In Figure 7-9, sublist 2 is partitioned using 74 as a pivot.

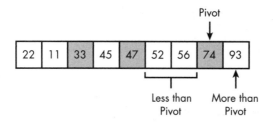

Figure 7-9: Partitioning sublist 2 of Figure 7-7

These partitions put both of their pivots in their correct sorted places in the list. The partitions also create four new sublists, as shown in Figure 7-10.

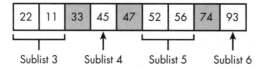

Figure 7-10: Now four sublists remain. Single-number sublists are trivial.

Sublists 4 and 6 contain a single number, which means there's nothing to partition. In Figure 7-11, sublists 3 and 5 are partitioned.

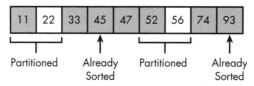

Figure 7-11: Only two trivial sublists remain, which means the whole list is sorted.

Now we have just two single-number sublists left, which means that the sort is complete.

In this example, the pivots evenly divided their partitions, but quicksort isn't always so lucky. Sometimes the split is uneven, and in the worst case, the pivot could be the lowest or highest number in the list, which means the partitioning produces the same result as a step in a selection sort. But most partitions will be roughly even, which tends to result in a much faster sort.

More generally, quicksort *scales* much better than selection sort. For any sorting method, sorting time increases as the size of the data collection increases, but selection sort slows down much more than quicksort. Let's say a particular computer can sort 10,000 records in around a second using either method. On the same computer, a selection sort of 1,000,000 records would take nearly 3 hours, while a quicksort would take only about 11 minutes.

Binary Search

When data is in order, software can find a particular record easily. One simple search method for ordered data is *binary search*. The word *binary* in this case doesn't refer to binary numbers, but to choosing between two alternatives.

Figure 7-12 shows binary search in action. The record we want has a key of 48. Initially, all we know is that the data in the collection is ordered on our key, so the record could appear anywhere. In step 1, we examine the record in the middle of the collection. If this record had a key of 48, we would we be done, but this is unlikely. However, because this record has a key of 62, which is larger than 48, we know that the desired record must appear among the first seven records. Thus, examining one record has eliminated not just that record from consideration, but also the seven records that appear later in the collection.

In step 2, we examine the fourth record, the midpoint of the remaining seven records. This record has a key of 23, which is lower than 48. Therefore the desired record must be in the three records between 23 and 62.

In step 3, we examine the middle of these remaining three records, which has a key of 47. This tells us the desired record must be the one record between 47 and 62. If that record did not have a key of 48, it would mean the collection did not include a record with that key.

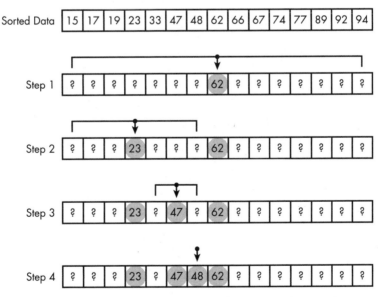

Figure 7-12: Binary search taking four steps to find a particular record in a collection of size 15

Each step in a binary search eliminates half of the records from consideration, which means binary search scales fantastically well. With a sequential search, doubling the size of a data collection doubles the time needed for the average search. With binary search, doubling the number of records requires just one more step. If we start with 31 records, for example, after examining the middle record, either we get lucky and find the desired record, or we find out whether the desired record is in the first or last 15 records. Either way we would now have only 15 records left to search, putting us back where we started in Figure 7-12. For huge data collections, the difference between binary and sequential search is dramatic. A sequential search of 1,000,000 records will examine 500,000 records on average, while a binary search of 1,000,000 records will examine no more than 20.

Indexing

To keep the figures simple, our examples to this point have used just record keys. In practice, though, the rest of the record has to be stored somewhere, and this can cause problems. To see why, we have to understand the choice software faces when allocating storage space for data, whether in main memory, on a hard drive, or anywhere else.

Fixed-size storage allocation assigns each record the same amount of space and is used for data that is either always the same size or has a small maximum size. Credit card numbers, for example, are always 16 digits. The names of credit card owners, on the other hand, vary in size, but there are only so many letters that will fit on the card. Both card numbers and cardholder names could be stored in a fixed number of bytes. In Figure 7-13, the maximum size of a last name is 15 characters, just long enough for Hammond-Hammond. The other names are shorter, resulting in wasted bytes, shown as shaded squares. Because the space needed to store a name is small, though, this wasted space is of no great concern.

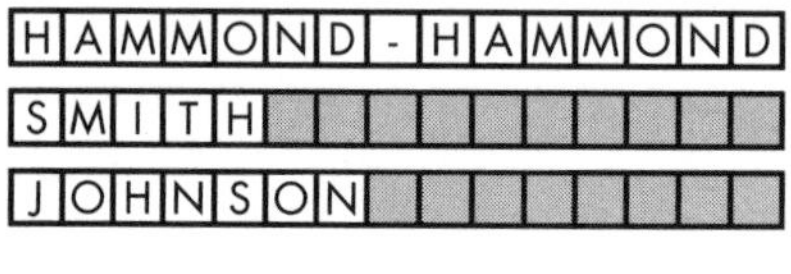

Figure 7-13: Fixed allocation of storage results in wasted space

Variable-size storage allocation exactly fits the data. Consider a collection of MP3 files. Roughly speaking, the longer the song, the larger the MP3 file. A short pop song might be 3 or 4MB, while a progressive-rock epic might be as large as 20MB. We wouldn't want to store song data in fixed space because this would waste too much space for shorter songs, and this would limit the length of a song. Instead, the data should be stored in just as much space as needed.

Variable-size storage allocation uses space efficiently, but fixed-size storage allocation is required for software to use efficient search methods. When all the records in a collection are the same size, software can quickly find a record in a particular position.

This is because storage locations are identified by numerical *addresses*. Every byte in digital storage—whether in a computer's main memory, or on a flash drive or hard drive—can be precisely located by its address. If a computer has 8GB of main memory, for example, those bytes are numbered from zero to just over eight trillion. Collections of fixed-size records are stored contiguously, which makes finding a record's address simple. Suppose a collection has 100 records, each 20 bytes in size, and the collection begins at address 1,000. That puts the first record at address 1,000, the second at 1,020, the third at 1,040, and so on. We can calculate the address of any record by multiplying its position number by 20 and adding the result to 1,000. In this way, software can quickly locate any record in any collection of fixed-size records.

Finding records quickly is essential for a method like binary search. Without fixed-size records, the only way to find a record in a particular position is to start from the beginning of the data collection and count the records. That's just a sequential search, and defeats the point.

Choosing between fixed-size and variable-size storage allocation means choosing between efficient search and efficient storage. However, a technique called *indexing* gives us both. Indexing separates the keys from the rest of the records, much as a library card catalog allows patrons to search for books on cards before ultimately retrieving the books from the shelves.

An index is a table of record keys and addresses. The addresses themselves are stored as binary numbers with a fixed number of bits. For example, when Microsoft releases versions of Windows in "32-bit" and "64-bit" editions, those bit counts refer to the size of the addresses for main memory. Because the addresses are a fixed size, we can store the addresses and keys together in an index of fixed-size records that can be searched efficiently using a method like binary search. The rest of each record's data is stored in a variable-size allocation. This produces a data collection that is efficient for storage *and* searching.

Figure 7-14 shows an indexed data collection of four songs. On the left, the index contains the song titles and the addresses for the remaining data of each song, such as the artist name and the encoded music. On the right is a block of memory cells numbered from 1 to 400. The arrows point to each address.

As shown in the example, this split data allocation allows each record to use as much or as little space as needed. It even allows the index and remaining data to be on different storage devices. For example, the index might be kept in a computer's fast main memory, while the encoded music data is left on its relatively slow hard drive. Because only the index is needed for search, such an arrangement allows for efficient search while using the minimum amount of main memory.

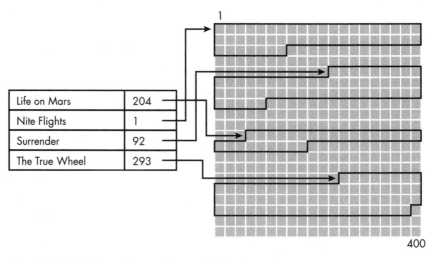

Life on Mars	204
Nite Flights	1
Surrender	92
The True Wheel	293

Figure 7-14: An indexed data collection of digital music

We can also have multiple indexes for the same data collection. The arrangement in Figure 7-14 allows individual songs to be quickly located by song title, but doesn't help us search for a song based on artist name or album title. Data collections can have multiple indexes for different search criteria, and because the main record data is simply referenced by an address, having multiple indexes doesn't greatly affect the total storage requirements for the data collection.

Hashing

Although ordered data is required for efficient searching, sorting data takes time. So far we've discussed sorting as though data collections need to be sorted just once. Sometimes that is the case; for example, a word processor needs a list of correctly spelled words for spell checking, but that list is created once and supplied as part of the application. A spellcheck word list is a *static* data collection, one that changes infrequently. However, many of the collections we search are *dynamic*—records are frequently added or removed. Because efficient searching requires ordered data, collections must be re-sorted following each addition or removal. When insertions and deletions are common, the time spent re-sorting the data collection can negate the benefit of a faster search. In such cases, it may be better to structure the data to facilitate frequent changes.

One data structure that eases additions and removals of records involves hash functions, which were introduced in Chapter 2. For this example let's imagine a hash function that produces a mere 3-bit hash, equivalent to a decimal number in the range of 0 to 7. We can use this to store records in a *hash table* with slots for 8 records. A *slot* is a place where a record could be stored.

To store a record in the hash table, we hash the record's key to determine which slot to use. Suppose we are storing MP3 files with song titles as the keys. Four titles and their associated hash codes are shown in Table 7-1.

Table 7-1: Hash Codes for Sample Song Titles

Song title	Hash code
Life on Mars	6
Nite Flights	4
Surrender	1
The True Wheel	4

Figure 7-15 shows the hash table after the insertion of the first three songs from Table 7-1. The first column in each record is a bit, which is 1 if the slot is in use and 0 if not. The second column is the title, and the third column holds the address of the remaining data.

0	0		
1	1	Surrender	(Address of Other Data Including Encoded Music)
2	0		
3	0		
4	1	Nite Flights	(Address of Other Data Including Encoded Music)
5	0		
6	1	Life on Mars	(Address of Other Data Including Encoded Music)
7	0		

Figure 7-15: An eight-slot hash table

The beauty of a hash table is that a search doesn't really require searching. We just run the key through the hash function and the result tells us where the record should be. If there's no record in that slot, we know right away that the collection doesn't contain a record with that key. Even better, hash tables avoid the effort of sorting. This makes a hash table an excellent choice for a collection with frequent additions and deletions of records.

However, we haven't inserted the fourth song in the list. The song title "The True Wheel" hashes to 4, the same number as "Nite Flights." As you may remember from Chapter 2, a hash function is not guaranteed to produce a different hash value for every input, and indeed, some matching hash values, or *collisions*, are inevitable. Since we can put only one record in a slot, we need a rule for handling collisions. The simplest rule is to use the first empty slot after the collision point. Because slot 4 is already occupied with "Nite Flights," we would place "The True Wheel" in the next open slot, which is slot 5, as shown in Figure 7-16.

0	0		
1	1	Surrender	(Address of Other Data Including Encoded Music)
2	0		
3	0		
4	1	Nite Flights	(Address of Other Data Including Encoded Music)
5	1	The True Wheel	(Address of Other Data Including Encoded Music)
6	1	Life on Mars	(Address of Other Data Including Encoded Music)
7	0		

Figure 7-16: Resolving a collision. The second song that hashes to 4 is placed in the next empty slot, which is slot 5.

This handles the collision problem, but it complicates the use of the hash table.

With this collision rule in place, finding a record is no longer a one-step process. Each search still starts at the slot indicated by the hash code, but then checks the slots one by one until it finds the matching song title. If the search reaches an empty slot, the song isn't in the collection.

Collisions can also cause records to be stored far from the position indicated by the hash code. For example, if a title with a hash code of 5 is inserted into the table shown in Figure 7-16, even though no previous song title has hashed to 5, the slot is already filled by "The True Wheel," and the new song would move all the way to slot 7. As a hash table fills, these situations become more common, degrading search performance; in effect, some hash table searches become miniature sequential searches.

Collisions also complicate the deletion of records. Suppose "Nite Flights" is removed from the hash table of Figure 7-16. The obvious way to remove a record is just to mark the slot "empty" again, but that doesn't work. To see why, remember that the song title "The True Wheel" hashed to 4, and the song was stored in slot 5 only because slot 4 was occupied at the time. A search for "The True Wheel" will begin at slot 4 as indicated by the hash code, find the slot empty, and end the search unsuccessfully. The song is still in the index table, but can't be found by a hash search.

To avoid this problem, we can remove the song data but keep the slot marked as occupied, as shown in Figure 7-17.

Slot 4 is now what is called a *tombstone*. By leaving the slot marked as occupied while deleting the data, we ensure that searches still work. However, tombstones waste space. Furthermore, because the table never really frees any record slots, the performance issues of congestion remain.

For these reasons, hash tables are periodically *rehashed*. Once a certain percentage of the slots in a table are occupied, a new, larger table is created, and each key in the original table is hashed with a new hash function, producing a fresh, sparsely populated table without any tombstones.

0	0		
1	1	Surrender	(Address of Other Data Including Encoded Music)
2	0		
3	0		
4	1		
5	1	The True Wheel	(Address of Other Data Including Encoded Music)
6	1	Life on Mars	(Address of Other Data Including Encoded Music)
7	0		

Figure 7-17: Leaving slot 4 marked as occupied after deletion of its data

Web Search

All of the techniques shown in this chapter are needed for efficiently searching large data collections, and no collection is larger than the Web. A search engine such as Google depends upon a vast index, where the keys are search terms, the addresses are URLs, and the web pages are the records. The size of the Google index is estimated at around 100 petabytes, or 100,000,000 gigabytes. To find something in an index this large requires all of the best search techniques. Although these techniques help illustrate how an index this large could be searched, they don't tell us how the index was created in the first place.

Search engines use *robots*, programs that run without direct human intervention, to build their indexes. The robots crawl all over the Web. Starting at some particular web page, they make a list of all the links on that page. Those linked pages are then processed to find links to other pages, and so on. Eventually the robot has links to most of the content on the Web.

Some content, though, is more difficult to locate. Some pages can't be reached from a site's home page but are instead found through the site's own search engine. A news site, for example, may not link to older articles but does provide a local search for its archives. This unlinked but valuable content is known as the *deep web*. Incorporating deep web content into a search engine index usually requires some assistance from the site. Site managers have several ways to provide web-crawling robots a "table of contents" for all the pages on the site, such as a document called a *Sitemap*. This document is named after the *site map* page some sites provide for users to quickly find the content they are looking for, but has a specific format that's easy for robots to process. Sitemaps keep search engines updated with content changes and are especially useful for sites with deep content that would otherwise be left out of search engine indexes.

Ranking Results

As robots gather pages, search engines mine the pages for keywords, counting how often each keyword appears on each page. Early search engines employed little more than a list of keywords along with their page counts. If you searched for *cake*, the page where *cake* most often appeared would be at the top of the returned list. That's logical enough, but a mere word count doesn't produce what we now consider to be good search results.

The first problem is that it's too easy for someone to exploit the system for personal gain. Suppose the operator of a site selling knockoff pharmaceuticals wants to get a lot of traffic and doesn't care how it's done. When the operator discovers that legions of people are searching for *omelette recipe*, the operator might put those words on the home page as many times as possible, even hiding the words in the behind-the-scenes formatting code. As a result, the site might be among the first returned on searches for omelette recipes, even though no such recipes appear on the site. Word counts do not guarantee a match between search terms and content.

Another website operator might build a site that is legitimately about omelettes, but it's filled with content stolen from Wikipedia, in order to generate revenue from ads about a zero-cholesterol egg substitute. In this case, the word count correctly connects the search term to matching content, but the quality of the content is poor.

The underlying issue is that the websites are self-reporting the nature and the quality of their content. What's missing is the opinion of a disinterested viewer. Ideally, search engines could employ an army of reviewers to determine what pages are about and how well they cover their chosen topics. The Web is so vast and ever-changing, though, that this is a practical impossibility.

Instead, search engines rely on the opinions of other websites. They acquire these opinions in the form of *inbound links*. The number of links to a particular page is a good metric for how that page is regarded by the online community. In Figure 7-18, page C has four inbound links, page D has none, and each of the others has one. On this basis alone, page C appears to be the most valued resource, while A, B, and E appear equally useful.

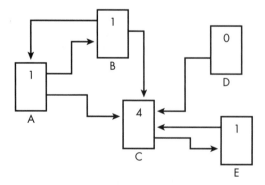

Figure 7-18: The number of links pointing to a page is one factor used by search engines to determine ranking.

There's more to the story though. A page with a high inbound link count grants more points to the pages it links to. In the previous figure, three pages have only one inbound link, but the quality of each link is different. Page E is linked from page C, which has a high inbound link count, while pages A and B are linked only from each other. Factoring the quality of each link into the link count helps to foil *link farming*, in which large numbers of pointless websites are created, often through free host services, for the purpose of increasing a target site's inbound link count.

In effect, this turns the Web into a collection of self-organized expert communities. When a number of well-regarded cooking sites begin linking to a new omelette-focused site, which in turn links back to omelette-related content in the established sites, the new site is inducted into the online cooking community. Thereafter, the new site's links count as much as the older, established sites.

Using the Index Effectively

While building the index is the bulk of the work of making a search engine, how the index is used during a search is just as important. Good search results require attention to detail.

For one thing, a search engine cannot merely use the supplied search terms as keywords. Consider the differences in word forms. You might type *frozen rain* in a search box, but most pages with relevant information use the form *freezing rain*. By linking together different forms of keywords in its index, a search engine can maximize the usefulness of results. This idea applies to synonymous terms as well. Because the words *insomnia* and *sleeplessness* mean the same thing, searching for either term produces similar results, even though some pages predominantly use one word or the other. For example, the Wikipedia article on insomnia appears in the first few results for either search term, even though, at the time of this writing, the word *sleeplessness* appears only twice in the article, while the word *insomnia* appears over 200 times.

The results from these search terms are not identical, though. A search for *insomnia* will also include links to the 2002 film *Insomnia*, but these links aren't returned by a search for *sleeplessness*. That result makes sense—presumably, no one searching for the film would have entered a synonym of the film's title—but how can a search engine know the two terms are linked in some ways but not others?

Tracking how search terms are combined can yield valuable clues. If searchers frequently add the terms *movie* or *film* to the term *insomnia*, then searches for just *insomnia* may indicate someone interested in the film and not the medical condition.

Furthermore, the links on a search results page are not actually direct links to the listed pages. Instead, they are *pass-through links*. For example, if you search Google for *insomnia*, then click on the link for the Wikipedia entry, you'll first be taken to the google.com server, which will then redirect you to wikipedia.org. Google tracks which result you selected, and this data, collected from countless users over time, allows Google to fine-tune the results, keeping the links that users actually find useful near the top.

Search engines can also make use of the location of the person searching. For example, when you search for *smiley's pizza* while you're standing in a particular town, the search engine appends the town's name to the search, so that the results are localized, instead of returning the websites of the most popular pizzerias with that name in the entire world.

What's Next for Web Search

As impressive as current web search capabilities are, there's still room for improvement.

For example, images provide unique challenges for search engines. Currently, image files are indexed based on accompanying text. A search engine might gather clues from an image's filename, or make educated guesses based on the text surrounding the image on the page.

We can soon expect the use of *computer vision* techniques in web indexes. Such software techniques transform an image into a description of the image. In some ways this is the reverse of the graphics techniques described in Chapters 4 and 5, where mathematical models were rendered into images. With computer vision, images are simplified into mathematical descriptions that are then categorized by pattern. Such software is currently used in self-governing robots, so that they can recognize an object they have been sent to retrieve. Future search engines may process the Web's images using these techniques, identifying both general subjects ("clear sky," "kittens") and specific subjects ("Eiffel Tower," "Abraham Lincoln") within the images.

Indexes will also be updated faster. Currently web indexes update only when a web-crawling robot passes through. In the future, indexes may be updated in near real time, so that conversations quickly developing throughout social media can be indexed as they happen. Eventually, real-time search may be combined with artificial intelligence to automatically generate basic news stories from social media for fast-breaking events like natural disasters.

But those are tomorrow's marvels. The Web and its search engines are the marvel of today, a powerhouse of information unfathomable just a few decades ago.

8

CONCURRENCY

Usually we can tell when software is doing something interesting, even if we don't know how it's done. We know that computers make graphics, encrypt our transmissions, and stream our videos. What we miss, though, is that these tasks often involve multiple programs, multiple processors, or even multiple computers connected via a network, accessing the same data at the same time.

This overlapping access of data, known as *concurrency*, is a vital part of modern technology. High-performance tasks like graphics and shared resources like websites wouldn't be possible without it. But concurrency causes big problems when it's not carefully managed. In this chapter, we'll see how results can become scrambled when multiple processors access the same data. Then we'll look at the clever software (and hardware) techniques that keep processors from getting in each other's way.

Why Concurrency Is Needed

Situations that require concurrency fall into three basic categories: performance, multiuser environments, and multitasking.

Performance

Concurrency is needed when there's more work to do than a single processor can handle. Until recently, the number of instructions a processor could execute in a second was steadily increasing, but now the pace of improvement has slowed. In order to execute more instructions in the same amount of time, a processor has to run faster. The faster it runs, the more power courses through it and the hotter it gets, which can eventually damage the components.

To mitigate that problem, the size of the components in the processor keeps getting smaller so that they draw less current and remain relatively cool. But it's getting difficult to make processor components any smaller, which in turn makes it difficult to make them run any faster. When a single processor can't get the job done, the only solution is to use multiple processing cores. We saw this with video game graphics in Chapter 5, but it's not just high-end game graphics that need multiple processors. Even today's basic graphics tasks may require multiple processor cores.

Multiuser Environments

Concurrency also allows networked computer systems to work together. Suppose you are playing an online game such as *World of Warcraft*. The game tracks each player's actions as well as those of the computer-controlled monsters. The game's servers tally every spell and axe swing, and calculate the damage done, the monsters slain, and the loot dropped.

Concurrency is required here because the processor in every player's computer must share the data of nearby players and computer-controlled creatures.

Multitasking

Concurrency can occur even in situations where only one processor is involved. Modern computers *multitask*, which means they are constantly switching between different programs, even when we think we're doing only one thing on the computer at a time. For example, multitasking is what allows your email client to receive a new message while you surf the Web. In these cases, whether or not the computer has multiple processor cores, it's definitely running multiple *processes*—different programs with overlapping executions.

Printing is another typical example. When you print a recipe from a website, the software that manages the printer, known as the driver, collects the print data in an orderly queue and then passes it on to the printer as needed. This is called *print spooling*. Without print spooling, the browser could send the data only as fast as the printer processed it, which means that you would have to wait for the print job to finish before you could do anything else with the browser.

Print spooling can't work without concurrency. You can think of a print spool as one of those carousels that sit in the window between the front counter and the kitchen in a short-order restaurant, like the one shown in Figure 8-1. Someone in the front puts new orders on the carousel, and someone in the back takes down the orders as they are fulfilled. The shared data storage of the carousel allows the order takers and the cooks to work independently.

Existing Orders Retrieved in Back

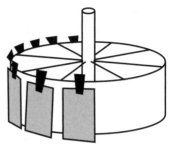

New Orders Added in Front

Figure 8-1: An order-ticket carousel

This arrangement is known as a *shared buffer* and is frequently used behind the scenes in software. For example, suppose you are typing an email, but your computer momentarily slows down so that nothing you typed appears on screen. Then the system catches up, and everything you typed is now in the email. That happens because the keyboard doesn't communicate directly with the email program, but uses the operating system as an intermediary. The operating system queues the keystrokes in a shared buffer so the email program can access them when ready.

Multitasking also allows programs to sit in the background and interrupt you when something significant happens. When a new email alert appears in the corner of your desktop's screen while you are working in a word processor, or your phone signals a newly received text message while you're playing a game, that's multitasking at work.

Beyond the performance benefits of multiple processors and distributed processing, the importance of multitasking means some form of concurrency is required to provide the basic computing functionality we rely on daily.

How Concurrency Can Fail

Although concurrency is a vital part of everyday computing, it creates enormous headaches for software and can produce serious problems if proper safeguards aren't in place to prevent them.

The underlying issue is how data is copied when it's used in calculations. Essentially, all a computer processor does is retrieve numbers from storage and either perform math with them or compare them. To do these tasks, though, it must copy the numbers from wherever they are stored to locations inside the processor. Stored data isn't changed directly. Instead, the computer fetches the value from main memory, or a hard drive, or across a network, and delivers it to the innermost part of the processor. The processor performs the math on this internal copy, and then sends the updated value back to storage to replace the original data.

Suppose you're playing a first-person shooter game. You have 300 bullets in reserve when you run over an ammo clip, picking up 20 more bullets. Figure 8-2 shows the steps involved. To update your bullet count, the processor first retrieves your current bullet count and the number of bullets in the clip from their places in storage, shown in step 1. These values are fed into the inputs of an "adder" circuit in the processor, as shown in step 2, which performs the actual math. Then the result is sent back to main memory, replacing the old value in the bullet count storage location, as shown in step 3.

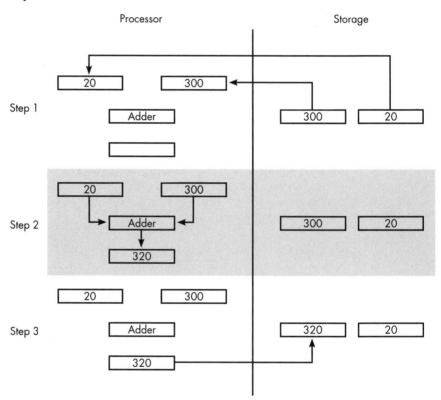

Figure 8-2: Three steps to update a number from 300 to 320

This update sequence causes problems when multiple processes attempt to make alterations to the same storage location. Take, for example, a *massively multiplayer online game (MMO)*. Trina Orcslayer and Skylar Rockguardian are two players. They are both officers of the same "guild," and this game allows guilds to hold shared bank accounts across multiple game servers. On Friday morning, the balance of the guild account is exactly 10,000 gold, and Skylar and Trina each have 500 gold in their personal accounts. Sometime that day, Skylar withdraws 300 gold from the guild account while Trina deposits 200 gold into it. If these are the only transactions that happen, the final balance should be 9,900 in the guild account (10,000 − 300 + 200), 800 in Skylar's account (500 + 300), and 300 in Trina's account (500 − 200).

And that's what will happen if the transactions are kept separate. Suppose Skylar makes the withdrawal in the morning, and Trina makes her deposit that afternoon. We won't get into programming here, but let's consider the steps that the game software will take to carry out these transactions. Let's start with Skylar's withdrawal:

1. Retrieve the balance of the guild account. Call this **Skylar's copy**.
2. Subtract 300 gold from **Skylar's copy**.
3. Add 300 gold to Skylar's personal stash.
4. Update the guild bank balance to **Skylar's copy**.

Now suppose Trina makes the deposit in the afternoon. The steps of her transaction are:

1. Retrieve the balance of the guild account. Call this **Trina's copy**.
2. Subtract 200 gold from Trina's personal stash.
3. Add 200 gold to **Trina's copy**.
4. Update the guild bank balance to **Trina's copy**.

In this example everything works fine. But what happens if Skylar and Trina perform their transactions at the same time? In that case, the final balance of the guild account could be incorrect. This happens if the original guild balance of 10,000 gold is retrieved for calculation by both processes before either of them completes the transaction.

Take a look at the details shown in Table 8-1. When Trina and Skylar initiate transactions at the same time, the same 10,000 balance is retrieved into their separate copies of the balance. Trina's copy is increased to 10,200, while Skylar's copy is decreased to 9,700. Then both of the updated figures overwrite the guild account balance. In the example shown in the table, Skylar's updated number arrives last, which means 9,700 is the new account balance and 200 gold has simply vanished.

It could have worked out the other way—Trina's copy could have arrived after Skylar's, increasing the guild's gold balance, but of course neither result is correct. The only correct final balance is 9,900 gold, the balance that corresponds to the two transactions occurring separately.

Situations similar to this example are possible whenever two or more processes use the same data simultaneously. The general term for this situation is a *race condition*, since all the processes involved are racing to complete their task first. In this case the process that finishes last "wins," because it determines the final value of the data.

While this example features two different processors, Trina's and Skyler's, it's important to note that race conditions can happen even with a single processor. Because multitasking involves switching the processor to a different program many times a second, multiple processes operating on the same data could interleave, creating a race condition.

Table 8-1: The Danger of Overlapping Bank Transactions

Step	Description	Skylar's copy	Trina's copy	Guild balance
Trina 1	Retrieve the guild balance from the bank.		10,000	10,000
Skylar 1	Retrieve the guild balance from the bank.	10,000		10,000
Trina 2	Subtract 200 gold from Trina's stash.		10,000	10,000
Trina 3	Add 200 gold to Trina's copy of the guild balance.		10,200	10,000
Skylar 2	Subtract 300 gold from Skylar's copy of the guild balance.	9,700		10,000
Skylar 3	Add 300 gold to Skylar's stash.	9,700		10,000
Trina 4	Send Trina's copy of the guild balance to the bank.		10,200	10,200
Skylar 4	Send Skylar's copy of the guild balance to the bank.	9,700		9,700

Making Concurrency Safe

In order to make concurrency useful, then, we need to prevent race conditions. This requires enforcing rules on how processes can access data. The tighter the restrictions, the easier it is to prevent problems from occurring, but these restrictions can have an adverse effect on performance.

Read-Only Data

One possible restriction is to allow processes to retrieve data simultaneously, but prohibit them from changing it; this is known as *read-only* data. This eliminates the possibility of a race condition but at an enormous cost. Most applications that require shared data access simply can't work without the ability to change the data. So this method is rarely considered. However, as we'll see later, distinguishing which processes want to change data from those that merely want to read data can improve the performance of concurrency.

Transaction-Based Processing

Another straightforward, comprehensive solution eliminates simultaneous data access entirely. The race condition occurs in the example because Skylar's and Trina's transactions overlap. What if we prevent overlapping transactions? To enforce this rule, once any bank transaction begins, we wait for it to signal its completion before any other transaction may start. For example, the steps in Skylar's process now might look like this:

1. Signal **Start Transaction** to the bank server.
2. Retrieve the balance of the guild account. Call this **Skylar's copy**.
3. Subtract 300 gold from **Skylar's copy**.
4. Add 300 gold to Skylar's personal stash.
5. Update the guild bank balance to **Skylar's copy**.
6. Signal **End Transaction** to the bank server.

The steps in Trina's process would be likewise bracketed:

1. Signal **Start Transaction** to the bank server.
2. Retrieve the balance of the guild account. Call this **Trina's copy**.
3. Subtract 200 gold from Trina's personal stash.
4. Add 200 gold to **Trina's copy**.
5. Update the guild bank balance to **Trina's copy**.
6. Signal **End Transaction** to the bank server.

The bank server process enforces the transaction rules. When no transaction is under way, a signal to start a new transaction is immediately accepted. So if Trina's transaction began during an idle period, it would continue. If, however, the *start transaction* signal from Skylar's process arrived while Trina's transaction was being processed, Skylar's transaction would have to wait until Trina's transaction finished. And if other transactions arrived during this time, the bank server would put them in a queue, to process them in the order in which they arrived.

This rule transforms the guild bank into the equivalent of a lobby with a single teller. If a customer arrives and the teller is available, the customer gets immediate service; otherwise, the customer must wait until the teller is free. This prevents race conditions but robs the system of the performance benefit of having multiple processors. Just as having one teller in a busy bank means a long wait for each customer, allowing only one transaction through the bank server at a time means a relatively long wait for each transaction.

The rule is much too strict. At any given time, the bank may be handling a large number of transactions, and few (if any) of them involve the same accounts. This rule prevents race conditions by preventing all overlapping transactions, even when the overlap is harmless.

Semaphores

Another idea takes advantage of the fact that most of the transactions are not interacting with the same data. If the transaction rule is like a bank with a single teller, a better rule would be like a bank where every account has its own personal teller. Two or more customers attempting to access the same account at the same time will form a queue, but customers accessing different accounts won't slow each other down at all.

The secret ingredient behind this technique is a special type of data called a *semaphore*. In nautical language, semaphores are flags that ships hoist to signal other ships; in software, semaphores are the numerical equivalent of flags, signaling whether or not logically connected data is in use. The simplest type of semaphore has just two possible values, 0 or 1, and is called a *binary semaphore*.

How Semaphores Prevent Race Conditions

Returning to our guild bank account, we can avoid the race condition by creating semaphores on the bank server for each of the account balances. Each semaphore begins with a value of 1.

Before requesting an account balance, a process must first *acquire* the semaphore associated with that account. This acquire operation will check the value of the semaphore. If the semaphore is 1, it means no other process is using the associated balance; in this case, the semaphore changes to 0, and the process will be allowed to continue.

If the semaphore is already 0, though, it means another process is currently accessing the associated balance. In this case, the software will have to wait.

When a process completes its transaction, it *releases* the semaphore, which immediately sets its value back to 1. This allows one of the processes waiting for the semaphore to continue.

Using semaphores, Skylar's process would look like this:

1. **Acquire** the semaphore for the guild account.
2. Retrieve the balance of the guild account. Call this **Skylar's copy**.
3. Subtract 300 gold from **Skylar's copy**.
4. Add 300 gold to Skylar's personal stash.
5. Update the guild bank balance to **Skylar's copy**.
6. **Release** the semaphore for the guild account.

And Trina's:

1. **Acquire** the semaphore for the guild account.
2. Retrieve the balance of the guild account. Call this **Trina's copy**.
3. Subtract 200 gold from Trina's personal stash.
4. Add 200 gold to **Trina's copy**.
5. Update the guild bank balance to **Trina's copy**.
6. **Release** the semaphore for the guild account.

In this way, Skylar and Trina are prevented from accessing the guild balance at the same time, preventing the race condition. Additionally, neither transaction will affect any other transaction that doesn't deal with this particular account.

How Semaphores Are Made

Now let's look at how semaphores are actually made. If semaphores aren't implemented with care, they can produce the very race conditions they are intended to prevent. Although the acquire operation is just one step for Skylar's and Trina's processes, in reality, it takes several steps itself:

1. Retrieve the value of the semaphore.
2. If the value is 0, go back to step 1 and try again.
3. Set the semaphore to 0.

Now consider what happens if both Skylar's and Trina's processes attempt to acquire the guild account semaphore at the same time. If the semaphore had a value of 1, both processes could retrieve this initial value (in step 1) before either had a chance to check the value and set it to 0. In this case, both processes would think that they were the only process that had acquired the semaphore, and were therefore free to do whatever they wanted with the accompanying bank balance. We're right back where we started.

To make a semaphore, then, software needs some help from hardware. The processor on the bank server must be able to implement the acquire and release operations in such a way that nothing can interrupt them. This is known as making the operations *atomic*, which in this sense means indivisible.

Modern processors implement a hardware operation known as *test-and-set*. This sets a byte in main memory to a particular value, while retrieving the previous value for inspection. Test-and-set makes semaphores possible. In the list of semaphore steps, the problem is the potential interruption between steps 1 and 3. If two different processes execute the first step before either reaches the third step, both will be able to alter the data that the semaphore is supposed to protect. Using the atomic test-and-set operation, though, a semaphore acquire operation can be implemented like this:

1. Using test-and-set, set the semaphore to 0 and retrieve the old value.
2. If the old value was 0, go back to step 1 and try again.

Now the race condition cannot happen. If two processes attempt to acquire the same semaphore at the same time, they will each execute the test-and-set in step 1. Both operations will set the semaphore value to 0, but only the semaphore that tests-and-sets first will retrieve a 1. The other process will retrieve a 0. One process will immediately continue, while the other will have to wait.

The Problem of Indefinite Waits

A process acquiring a semaphore using this two-step plan—continuously checking the semaphore's value until it changes back to 1—is said to be in a *spin lock*. This is the simplest way to wait for a semaphore to become available, but it has two major problems. First, it wastes processor time. A process in a spin lock is continuously executing code, but the code isn't doing anything useful. Secondly, spin locks can be unfair. In some cases, some processes cannot check the semaphore as fast as others. Perhaps the process is executing on a slower processor, or perhaps the process is communicating with a server across a slower network. Regardless of the reason, if a semaphore's resource is so popular that multiple processes are always waiting, a slower-checking process might never be able to snag the semaphore. This is known as *starvation*; picture the least-assertive person at a busy restaurant with only one waiter, and you'll get the idea.

Orderly Queues

Avoiding starvation requires a more organized approach to waiting. Banks organize the wait in their lobbies with cordons, forming groups of waiting customers into orderly queues. Semaphores can be designed to do the same thing. Rather than waste time continually checking the value of the semaphore, many acquire operations written so that when they do not succeed immediately, they put their process to sleep, so to speak. Putting a computer or phone to sleep means suspending all running applications in a way that allows the applications to be restored quickly. In the same way, if a process cannot immediately acquire a semaphore, it will be suspended and flushed out of the processor, but its internal data will remain in storage.

To accomplish this, the computer's operating system assigns each process a unique identification number. When an acquire operation has to wait, the process identifier is placed at the end of that semaphore's wait list. When the process currently holding that semaphore releases it, the first process on the list is awakened. In this way, processes acquire the semaphore in the same order they request it. A process may have to wait to acquire a popular semaphore, but will eventually get to the top of the list—it won't starve.

Starvation from Circular Waits

Although semaphores prevent race conditions when implemented and used correctly, they can cause starvation when processes need to access multiple pieces of data that are protected by semaphores.

Suppose Skylar and Trina's guild opens a second account that is accessible to lower-ranked guild officers, so now the guild has a main account and a secondary account. The banking system has implemented semaphores for each individual account, eliminating the chance of a race condition on any guild transactions.

But on a particular day, Skylar and Trina are each transferring 200 gold from one account to the other in opposite directions. Both transactions involve debiting one account and crediting the other. Skylar's transaction would have these steps:

1. **Acquire** the semaphore of the main account balance.
2. Retrieve the balance of the main account.

3. **Acquire** the semaphore of the secondary account balance.
4. Retrieve the balance of the secondary account.
5. Add 200 gold to the secondary account balance.
6. Subtract 200 gold from the main account balance.
7. Update the secondary account balance.
8. Update the main account balance.
9. **Release** the semaphore of the secondary account.
10. **Release** the semaphore of the main account.

Trina's transaction would run like this:

1. **Acquire** the semaphore of the secondary account balance.
2. Retrieve the balance of the secondary account.
3. **Acquire** the semaphore of the main account balance.
4. Retrieve the balance of the main account balance.
5. Add 200 gold to the main account balance.
6. Subtract 200 gold from the secondary account balance.
7. Update the main account balance.
8. Update the secondary account balance.
9. **Release** the semaphore of the main account.
10. **Release** the semaphore of the secondary account.

Because all shared value access is properly bracketed by the acquisition and release of associated semaphores, no race conditions can occur from the overlapping execution of these transactions. However, suppose both transactions begin around the same time and the first few steps interleave as shown in Table 8-2.

Table 8-2: Multiple Semaphores Leading to Indefinite Waiting

Step	Description	Main account semaphore	Secondary account semaphore
	Initial state.	1	1
Skylar 1	Acquire the semaphore of the main account balance.	0	1
Skylar 2	Retrieve the balance of the main account.	0	1
Trina 1	Acquire the semaphore of the secondary account balance.	0	0
Trina 2	Retrieve the balance of the secondary account.	0	0
Skylar 3	Acquire the semaphore of the secondary account balance.	0	0
Trina 3	Acquire the semaphore of the main account balance.	0	0

I've shown only these steps because these are the only steps that would occur. Both Skylar's and Trina's processes would halt at step 3, because both are trying to acquire semaphores that aren't available. What's worse is that they can never become available, because each is being held by the other process. This is like waiting for traffic to clear so you can turn left on a two-lane road, but someone going the other way wants to turn left behind you, as shown in Figure 8-3.

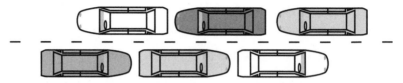

Figure 8-3: If both white cars are waiting to turn left, traffic is stopped.

Because neither process in this example can continue until the other process completes, this situation is known as a *circular wait*. In this case, the circular wait involves only two processes, but circular waits sometimes involve many processes, and is therefore difficult to detect or foresee. A circular wait is one form of *deadlock*, which describes a situation in which a process cannot be expected to continue. Circular waits are one way that concurrency can cause deadlocks, and unless precautions are taken, a circular wait can occur whenever processes hold multiple semaphores at once. Fortunately, such precautions can be easy to implement.

One solution is a rule by which semaphores must be acquired in some specified order. In our example, the game's bank management system can internally assign each account a number, and require processes to acquire account semaphores in numerical order. Or, put more broadly, a process can acquire an account's semaphore only when it does not currently hold a semaphore for an account with a higher number. This rule prevents the circular wait in the previous example. Let's suppose the main account is 39785 and the secondary account is 87685. Because the main account number is lower, both Skylar's and Trina's processes would attempt to acquire its semaphore first. If both processes tried at the same time, only one process would succeed. That process would then acquire the semaphore for the secondary account and complete the transaction, at which point both account semaphores would be released, allowing the other process to continue through completion.

Performance Issues of Semaphores

With the proper rules in place, semaphores enable concurrency without fear of race conditions, deadlock, or starvation. However, in situations where we are trying to boost performance by having multiple processors work together on the same job, enforcing these semaphore rules can limit the performance benefit we hoped to create. Instead of lots of processors working together, we are left instead with lots of processors waiting in line for an opportunity to work. Concurrent software can mitigate these performance issues by creating additional rules.

Sometimes a process needs access to a piece of data but doesn't need to change it. In our running guild bank example, suppose Skylar and Trina are both inspecting the main guild account at the same time—that is, neither player is depositing or withdrawing, but is merely checking the balance. In this case, no danger arises from the simultaneous access of the account. Even though the processes would have potentially overlapping retrieval operations, as long as neither one of them updated the balance, everything would be fine.

Allowing simultaneous access during "read-only" situations greatly improves multiprocessor performance, and requires only a modification of the semaphore concept. Instead of having one semaphore for each piece of data to be shared, we'll have two: a *read* semaphore and a *write* semaphore, subject to the following rules:

- Acquiring the associated *write* semaphore allows data to be retrieved or updated, just like how the semaphores worked in previous examples.
- Acquiring the associated *read* semaphore allows data to be retrieved, but not updated.
- A *write* semaphore can be acquired only when no process holds a semaphore (of either type) for that data.
- A *read* semaphore can be acquired only when no process holds a *write* semaphore for that data.

Following these rules means that at any given time, either one process will have acquired the write semaphore for a piece of data or one or more processes will have acquired read semaphores for that data. At first, this appears to be what we want. So long as processes are merely looking at, but not changing data, they can share access. Once a process needs to change the data, all other processes are locked out until the updating process completes its work.

Unfortunately, these rules potentially reintroduce the starvation problem. As long as read-only processes keep arriving, a process that needs a write semaphore might wait indefinitely. To prevent this from happening, we can modify the last rule as follows: "a read semaphore can be acquired only when no process is holding or waiting for a write semaphore." In other words, once a process attempts to acquire a write semaphore, all processes arriving later must wait behind it.

Another potential concern for performance is known as *granularity*, which in this context refers to whether we lock up individual pieces or collections of data. For example, the bank system could use semaphores to protect individual data elements, such as the balance of the main guild account, or it could apply a single read/write pair for all data related to a particular guild's finances, such as the balances of all guild accounts, the list of guild officers who are allowed to access that account, and so on.

Protecting data as a group can cause more waiting, because a process that may need only one or two numbers in a data group will have to lock up all the data in the group, potentially blocking another process that needs other, nonoverlapping data from the group. Very fine granularity can also hinder performance. Acquiring and releasing semaphores takes time, and with lots of semaphores, it's possible for processes to spend most of their time dealing with them. Developers must therefore carefully determine the best granularity for a particular application.

What's Next for Concurrency

For several reasons, we can expect concurrency to be an even greater concern for the future.

These days, multiple processing cores can be found even in our simplest computing devices. The push for more processing power will continue, and until the arrival of a new processing paradigm like quantum computing, more processing power will mean more processor cores.

Multitasking is now the norm. We expect our computing devices to run multiple applications at the same time, and to interrupt our foreground tasks when something interesting happens in the background.

Data and devices are becoming more connected than ever. Data and processing are increasingly being moved from client devices onto servers or clouds of interconnected servers. In computer gaming, socialization is the new paradigm, and in some games, even single-player game modes require an Internet connection.

In short, properly handling concurrency is becoming essential in everyday computing. What looks like a single computer running a single-user application may contain a multiprocessor that provides a multitasking environment with shared cloud storage for data. The vital power of concurrency is thus often invisible. As the trend toward even greater concurrency continues, we may take for granted the way in which so many processes work together without running into one another. But future improvements in computing depend upon further advancements in concurrency control. We don't know yet whether current methods of preventing deadlock, starvation, and race conditions will be sufficient as concurrency increases. If current methods are inadequate for solving future challenges, they will become the bottleneck until better methods are developed.

9

MAP ROUTES

Because we can instantly get directions using sites like Google Maps, we forget that not long ago people often got lost driving to unfamiliar destinations. Now software plans our route for us and even alters the route mid-trip if an accident or road closure blocks our way.

In computing, this task is called *finding the shortest path*. Despite the name, the goal isn't always to find the shortest path, but more generally to minimize the *cost*, where the definition of cost varies. If the cost is time, the software finds the fastest route. If the cost is distance, the software minimizes the mileage, truly finding the shortest path. By changing how cost is defined, the same software methods can find routes to match different goals.

What a Map Looks Like to Software

Although software can provide directions, it can't actually read a map. Instead, it uses tables of data. To see how we get from a map to a table of data, let's begin with Figure 9-1, which shows a portion of a city map for a simple routing problem. The goal is to find the quickest route from the corner of 3rd Street and West Avenue to the corner of 1st Street and Morris Avenue. The numbered arrows alongside the streets show the average driving time in seconds between intersections. Note that 1st Street and Morris Avenue are one-way streets.

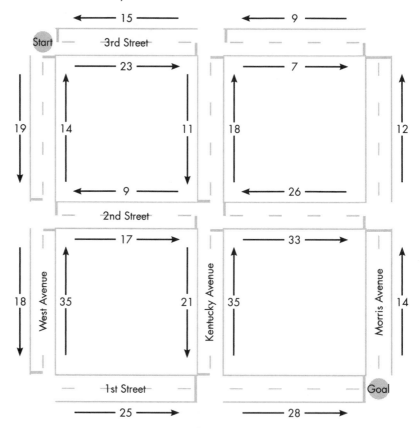

Figure 9-1: A simple routing problem: find the fastest route from 3rd and West to 1st and Morris.

To produce a data table that can be processed by software, we first reconceptualize the map as the *directed graph* shown in Figure 9-2. Here, the street intersections are represented as points labeled A through I. The arrows in Figure 9-1 become connections between points on the graph, known as *edges*.

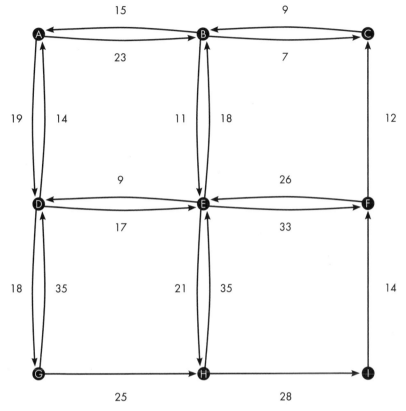

Figure 9-2: The map from Figure 9-1 as a directed graph

Using the directed graph, we put the data into the tabular form shown in Table 9-1. This table contains all of the information from the map in Figure 9-2 that software needs to find the fastest route. In Figure 9-2, for example, travel time from A to B is 23 seconds; the same information is provided by the first row of the table. Note that travel in impossible directions, such as from H to G, is not listed.

Table 9-1: The Data from the Directed Graph of Figure 9-2 in Tabular Form

From	To	Time
A	B	23
A	D	19
B	A	15
B	C	7
B	E	11
C	B	9
D	A	14
D	E	17

Table 9-1 *(continued)*

From	To	Time
D	G	18
E	B	18
E	D	9
E	F	33
E	H	21
F	C	12
F	E	26
G	D	35
G	H	25
H	E	35
H	I	28
I	F	14

Best-First Search

Now we're ready to find the quickest route on the map, which means finding the lowest-cost path from A to I on our graph. Many methods exist for solving this problem; the variation I'll describe is a type of algorithm called a *best-first search*. Calling this algorithm a "search" may be a little misleading, because this method doesn't aim for the destination. Instead, at each step it finds the best new route from the starting point to *any* point it hasn't already routed to. Eventually, this procedure stumbles upon a route to the destination, which will be the cheapest route possible from the start to the goal.

Here's how best-first search works for our example. All routes starting at A must first travel to either B or D. The algorithm starts by comparing these two choices, as shown in Figure 9-3.

In these figures, black circles mark the points we've found the best paths to, while gray circles indicate points we can reach directly from one of the marked (black) points. The numbers inside the circles represent the cost of the route to that point. In each step, the search examines all edges extending from marked to unmarked points to find the edge that produces the lowest-cost route. In this first step, the choice is between the A-to-B edge and the A-to-D edge. Because the travel time to D is less than the travel time to B, the lowest-cost route is from A to D, as shown in Figure 9-4.

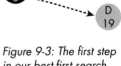

Figure 9-3: The first step in our best-first search. Starting from A, we can travel either to B or D.

We've just found the cheapest possible route from A to D. No matter what the rest of the graph looks like, it can't contain a lower-cost route from A to D, because this is the lowest-cost route of *all* routes starting from A. In the same way, each step will produce a new route that will be the lowest-cost route possible from A to some other point.

In the second step, there are four edges to consider: the A-to-B edge and the three edges extending from D. Again, the algorithm will choose the edge that creates the fastest new route. In considering the edges extending from D, we have to include the 19 seconds from A to D. For example, the time required to travel from A to E through D is the sum of the A-to-D edge time (19) and the D-to-E edge time (17), which is 36 seconds.

Note that one edge from D leads back to A. In Figure 9-4, the circle at the end of that edge is white to indicate that it will never be chosen. There's no benefit in taking a round trip back to our starting point. More generally, once a point has been included in a route (marked black in the figures), later appearances of that point are ignored, because a better route to it has already been found.

At this stage, the lowest-cost new route is made using the A-to-B edge. This brings us to the stage shown in Figure 9-5. Again, because we've found the lowest-cost route of all remaining routes, that makes this A-to-B route the fastest possible way to get from A to B.

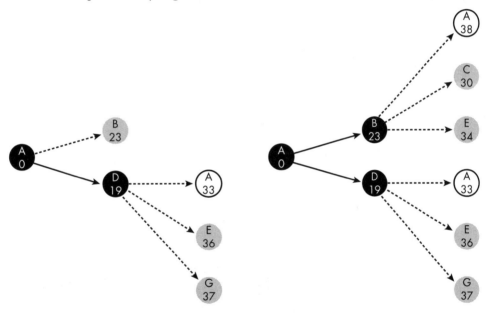

Figure 9-4: In the second step of our search, the best new route leads to D. Marking D exposes three new routing possibilities, one of which leads back to our starting point.

Figure 9-5: The third step in our best-first search finds the best route to point B.

We have six edges to consider next, although the edges leading back to A aren't contenders. The best choice uses the B-to-C edge to make an A-to-C route of 30 seconds, as shown in Figure 9-6.

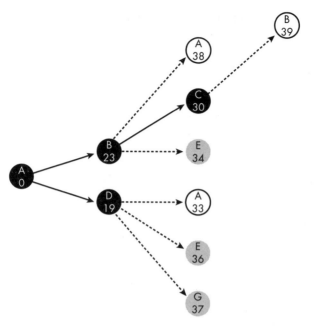

Figure 9-6: The fourth step in our search finds the best route to point C.

Finding the fastest route to C doesn't help us reach our ultimate goal, though. From C, we can only return to B, to which we already know the fastest route.

At this stage, the fastest new route is the one going through B to E, as shown in Figure 9-7.

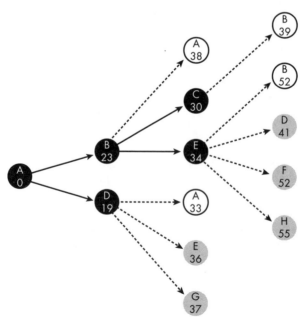

Figure 9-7: The fifth step in our best-first search finds the best route to E.

This process continues until we have reached the state shown in Figure 9-8. At this stage, the lowest-cost new route uses the edge from H to I, which means we've finally identified the best route from A to I.

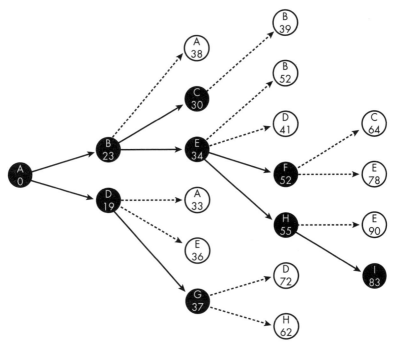

Figure 9-8: The ninth and final step in our best-first search reaches point I.

As shown, the fastest route from A to I is A-B-E-H-I. Looking at our original map in Figure 9-1 and its graph equivalent in Figure 9-2, we can see that this corresponds to taking 3rd Street to Kentucky Avenue, taking a left on 1st Street, and driving one block to our destination.

Reusing Prior Search Results

In this example, the best-first search found not only the fastest route from A to I, but also the fastest route to every other point on the map. Although this is an unusual result, the best-first process typically produces a surplus of information. At a minimum, the search results will also provide the best routes between intermediate points that lie along the route between the start and destination points. In our example, the best route from A to I contains the best routes from B to H, and from E to I, and so on. For this reason, the results of best-first searches can be stored for later use.

We can even use this data in searches involving points that weren't part of the original map data. To see why, consider Figure 9-9. This is the same directed graph in Figure 9-2 except that it includes a new point, J, that has edges to A and B.

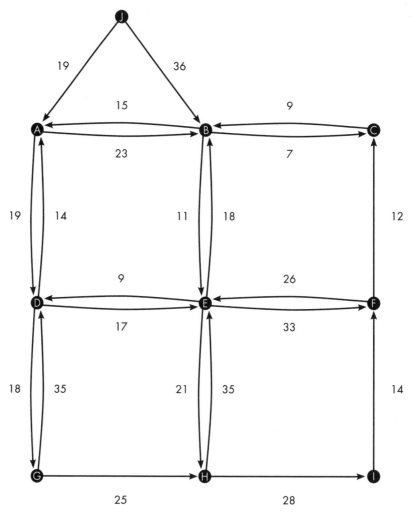

Figure 9-9: The directed graph from Figure 9-2 with an additional point, J

Suppose we need to find the fastest route from J to I. Any route from J begins by going to either A or B. We already know the fastest routes from A and B to I from the results in Figure 9-8. The fastest route from A to I takes 83 seconds. The fastest route from B to I takes 60 seconds; we find this by subtracting the A-to-B edge time of 23 seconds from the total A-to-I time of 83 seconds.

This means that the J-to-I route that starts by heading to A takes 102 seconds—19 seconds to reach A, and 83 seconds to follow the best route from A to I. The route that heads directly to B takes 96 seconds: 36 seconds to reach B, and 60 seconds from there to reach I. Using the previous search results makes finding the fastest J-to-I route much simpler.

Finding All the Best Routes at Once

In general, then, storing past search results benefits future searches. This idea can be extended to efficiently find the best routes between any two points on a given map, which is known as the *all-pairs shortest paths* problem.

Floyd's Algorithm

We'll solve the all-pairs shortest paths problem using *Floyd's algorithm* (sometimes called the *Floyd-Warshall algorithm*), which starts with simple routes of individual edges, then builds longer routes by connecting the existing routes using each point on the map in turn. This method uses a grid, the initial state of which is shown in Figure 9-10. At each step in the process, the grid contains the costs of the best routes between every pair of points. At the start, the only known routes are the edges that directly connect points, the same data from Figure 9-2 and Table 9-1. For example, the 23 in row A, column B, represents the cost of travel from A to B. The cost is 0 where the "from" and "to" points are the same.

from\to	A	B	C	D	E	F	G	H	I
A	0	23	-	19	-	-	-	-	-
B	15	0	7	-	11	-	-	-	-
C	-	9	0	-	-	-	-	-	-
D	14	-	-	0	17	-	18	-	-
E	-	18	-	9	0	33	-	21	-
F	-	-	12	-	26	0	-	-	-
G	-	-	-	35	-	-	0	25	-
H	-	-	-	-	35	-	-	0	28
I	-	-	-	-	-	14	-	-	0

Figure 9-10: The initial grid of numbers for Floyd's algorithm. At this stage the only routes in the grid are the direct connections between points.

As the process continues, this grid will be filled in and modified. New routes will be added where none initially exist, such as from A to F. Routes with lower costs will replace existing routes; if we can find a way to get from G to D in less than 35 seconds, for example, we'll replace the 35 currently in the grid.

We start by considering point A as a route connector. From Figure 9-10, we can see that B and D have routes to A. Because A has routes back to B and D, A can connect B to D and D to B. These new routes are shown as gray squares in Figure 9-11.

from \ to	A	B	C	D	E	F	G	H	I
A	0	23	-	19	-	-	-	-	-
B	15	0	7	34	11	-	-	-	-
C	-	9	0	-	-	-	-	-	-
D	14	37	-	0	17	-	18	-	-
E	-	18	-	9	0	33	-	21	-
F	-	-	12	-	26	0	-	-	-
G	-	-	-	35	-	-	0	25	-
H	-	-	-	-	35	-	-	0	28
I	-	-	-	-	-	14	-	-	0

Figure 9-11: Discovering new routes using point A as a connector

The cost of new routes is the sum of the costs of the two routes we are connecting. In Figure 9-11, the cost of the B-to-D route (34) is the cost of the B-to-A route (15) plus the cost of the A-to-D route (19), as indicated by the arrows. The cost of the D-to-B route (37) is computed the same way, as the sum of the D-to-A route (14) and the A-to-B route (23).

In the next step, we use point B to connect existing routes. This produces a whopping eight new routes, as shown in Figure 9-12.

from \ to	A	B	C	D	E	F	G	H	I
A	0	23	30	19	34	-	-	-	-
B	15	0	7	34	11	-	-	-	-
C	24	9	0	43	20	-	-	-	-
D	14	37	44	0	17	-	18	-	-
E	33	18	25	9	0	33	-	21	-
F	-	-	12	-	26	0	-	-	-
G	-	-	-	35	-	-	0	25	-
H	-	-	-	-	35	-	-	0	28
I	-	-	-	-	-	14	-	-	0

Figure 9-12: Discovering new routes using point B as a connector

As with the previous step, the cost of each new route is the sum of the costs of the two routes we are connecting. For example, the cost of the new A-to-E route (34) is the sum of the A-to-B cost (23) and the B-to-E cost (11).

In the next step, using C to connect existing routes reveals three new routes, as shown in Figure 9-13.

from\to	A	B	C	D	E	F	G	H	I
A	0	23	30	19	34	-	-	-	-
B	15	0	7	34	11	-	-	-	-
C	24	9	0	43	20	-	-	-	-
D	14	37	44	0	17	-	18	-	-
E	33	18	25	9	0	33	-	21	-
F	36	21	12	55	26	0	-	-	-
G	-	-	-	35	-	-	0	25	-
H	-	-	-	-	35	-	-	0	28
I	-	-	-	-	-	14	-	-	0

Figure 9-13: Discovering new routes using point C as a connector

In the next step, we have our first instance of a *better* route. Previously we found a 33-second route from E to A. In this step, we discover a 23-second route from E to A through D, and update the grid with the lower cost. Nine new routes are also found, bringing us to the state shown in Figure 9-14.

from\to	A	B	C	D	E	F	G	H	I
A	0	23	30	19	34	-	37	-	-
B	15	0	7	34	11	-	52	-	-
C	24	9	0	43	20	-	61	-	-
D	14	37	44	0	17	-	18	-	-
E	23	18	25	9	0	33	27	21	-
F	36	21	12	55	26	0	73	-	-
G	49	72	79	35	52	-	0	25	-
H	-	-	-	-	35	-	-	0	28
I	-	-	-	-	-	14	-	-	0

Figure 9-14: Discovering new routes using point D as a connector

This process continues, using the points E through I to connect routes in turn, resulting in the complete grid shown in Figure 9-15. By relating the points back to the street names on the original map, routing software can use this grid to provide the fastest time between any two locations on the map. If you want to know how many seconds it should take to get from the corner of 1st and West to the corner of 3rd and Morris, the software will translate this into a query about the G-to-C route on the graph. Then the answer can be found right there in the grid: 77 seconds.

from \ to	A	B	C	D	E	F	G	H	I
A	0	23	30	19	34	67	37	55	83
B	15	0	7	20	11	44	38	32	60
C	24	9	0	29	20	53	47	41	69
D	14	35	42	0	17	50	18	38	66
E	23	18	25	9	0	33	27	21	49
F	36	21	12	35	26	0	53	47	75
G	49	70	77	35	52	67	0	25	53
H	58	53	54	44	35	42	62	0	28
I	50	35	26	49	40	14	67	61	0

Figure 9-15: The complete grid produced by Floyd's algorithm, showing the fastest time possible from each point to every other point

Storing Route Directions

What this grid *doesn't* tell you, as you may have noticed, is what that fastest route is—only how much time it takes. For example, you can see that the fastest route from A to I takes 83 seconds, but does that route begin by going east or south, and where do you make the first turn? In order to record the route itself, we must record the initial direction of the routes when updating route times in the grid.

Figure 9-16 shows the starting grid. As before, the grid will be used to store the costs of the best routes found so far, but now it will also store the initial direction of travel for each route. This starting grid contains just the edges of the original graph. The 23 and B in the second column of the first row means the best route from A to B costs 23 and starts by heading toward B.

from \ to	A	B	C	D	E	F	G	H	I
A	0 -	23 B	- -	19 D	- -	- -	- -	- -	- -
B	15 A	0 -	7 C	- -	11 E	- -	- -	- -	- -
C	- -	9 B	0 -	- -	- -	- -	- -	- -	- -
D	14 A	- -	- -	0 -	17 E	- -	18 G	- -	- -
E	- -	18 B	- -	9 D	0 -	33 F	- -	21 H	- -
F	- -	- -	12 C	- -	26 E	0 -	- -	- -	- -
G	- -	- -	- -	35 D	- -	- -	0 -	25 H	- -
H	- -	- -	- -	- -	35 E	- -	- -	0 -	28 I
I	- -	- -	- -	- -	- -	14 F	- -	- -	0 -

Figure 9-16: The initial grid for Floyd's algorithm, amended to store the direction of travel for each route

In Figure 9-17, we use A to connect existing routes, as we did in Figure 9-11. But now, adding or updating a route in the grid means recording the direction as well. The new route from B to D, for example, begins by going to A. The logic is: "We've just discovered a route from B to D that goes through A. The fastest known route from B to A heads directly to A. Therefore, the route from B to D must also start by going to A."

from \ to	A	B	C	D	E	F	G	H	I
A	0 -	23 B	- -	19 D	- -	- -	- -	- -	- -
B	15 A	0 -	7 C	34 A	11 E	- -	- -	- -	- -
C	- -	9 B	0 -	- -	- -	- -	- -	- -	- -
D	14 A	37 A	- -	0 -	17 E	- -	18 G	- -	- -
E	- -	18 B	- -	9 D	0 -	33 F	- -	21 H	- -
F	- -	- -	12 C	- -	26 E	0 -	- -	- -	- -
G	- -	- -	- -	35 D	- -	- -	0 -	25 H	- -
H	- -	- -	- -	- -	35 E	- -	- -	0 -	28 I
I	- -	- -	- -	- -	- -	14 F	- -	- -	0 -

Figure 9-17: Discovering new routes using point A as a connector

Skipping over the steps for B and C, Figure 9-18 shows the grid just after we've added the routes for D. Here we've found a new route from B to G that takes 52 seconds. Because this new route goes through D, the route must begin the same way the route to D begins—by traveling to A.

from \ to	A	B	C	D	E	F	G	H	I
A	0 -	23 B	30 B	19 D	34 B	- -	37 D	- -	- -
B	15 A	0 -	7 C	34 A	11 E	- -	52 A	- -	- -
C	24 B	9 B	0 -	43 B	20 B	- -	61 B	- -	- -
D	14 A	37 A	44 A	0 -	17 E	- -	18 G	- -	- -
E	23 D	18 B	25 B	9 D	0 -	33 F	27 G	21 H	- -
F	36 C	21 C	12 C	55 C	26 E	0 -	73 C	- -	- -
G	49 D	72 D	79 D	35 D	52 D	- -	0 -	25 H	- -
H	- -	- -	- -	- -	35 E	- -	- -	0 -	28 I
I	- -	- -	- -	- -	- -	14 F	- -	- -	0 -

Figure 9-18: Discovering new routes using point D as a connector

Figure 9-19 shows the completed grid, with the times removed for clarity.

from \ to	A	B	C	D	E	F	G	H	I
A	-	B	B	D	B	B	D	B	B
B	A	-	C	E	E	E	E	E	E
C	B	B	-	B	B	B	B	B	B
D	A	E	E	-	E	E	G	E	E
E	D	B	B	D	-	F	D	H	H
F	C	C	C	E	E	-	E	E	E
G	D	D	D	D	D	H	-	H	H
H	E	E	I	E	E	I	E	-	I
I	F	F	F	F	F	F	F	F	-

Figure 9-19: The complete routing grid produced by Floyd's algorithm, showing the direction of travel. The fastest route from A to I is highlighted.

The fastest route from A to I is highlighted in the grid. We start at row A, column I, and see the fastest route from A to I starts by going to B. So then we look at row B and see the fastest route from B to I heads to E. The route from E heads to H, and the route from H reaches I. Using this grid is like stopping at every street corner and asking, "Which way should I turn?"

The Future of Routing

Today's software can provide accurate directions in an instant, so what can tomorrow's mapping software possibly do better?

Improvements in mapping will come from improvements in data. For example, if the software has access to hourly traffic data, it can tailor directions to the time of the trip.

Real-time traffic data may also be integrated into mapping software. For example, most mapping programs don't know about traffic issues until the user requests a new route. In the future, your mapping software may find out about accidents and road closures before you do and route you around the problems. Weather data may also be included to provide more accurate estimates of travel time, and to accommodate the preferences of drivers who wish to avoid driving in heavy rain or other troubling conditions.

Routing is just a small part of a larger area of software called *geographic information systems (GIS)*, which uses software to answer questions about maps and location-tagged data. Some GIS tasks have nothing to do with routing, such as determining if an area contains enough potential customers to support a new grocery store. But many interesting GIS projects combine the map routing concepts from this chapter with data about what's inside buildings along a map's roadways. By tracking where schoolchildren live, for example, GIS software can plan the most efficient routes for school buses.

In the future, routing software may expand to encompass more of the abilities of general GIS tools. When you need a route for a long drive out of town, the software may not provide just the turns you need to take, but also highlight places where you might want to stop, like the best-priced gas stations and the restaurants that serve your favorite food.

INDEX

GPU (graphics processing unit), 87, 90
granularity, 173
graph, directed. *See* directed graph
graphics accelerator, 86
graphics processing unit (GPU), 87, 90
group of pictures, 138

H

H.264 standard, 143
handshaking, 52–54
hash chaining, 29–31
    chain merging, 31
    reduction function, 29, 31
hash table, 29, 31
hashing, 20–23, 154–156
    avalanche, 17, 21
    collision, 20, 26
    desirable properties, 20–21
    digital signature. *See* digital signature
    encoded password, 21
    irreversibility, 20, 25
    iterative, 32–33
    keyed, 55
    MAC, 55
    MD5. *See* MD5
    reduction function, 29, 31
    rehashing, 156
    salt, 34, 35
    slot, 154
    tombstone, 156
height map, 106
HTTPS, 52–56
    authority, 53
    certificate, 53
    handshaking, 52–54
    issuer, 53
    MAC, 55
    master secret, 54
    premaster secret, 53
    security of, 55–56
    session, 52
    transmission, 54–56
Huffman encoding, 120, 142
    code creation, 120
    in JPEG, 134

I

IDCT (inverse discrete cosine
      transform), 127
I-frame, 138, 139
images
    digital, 51–60
    searching for, 160

inbound link, 158
indexing, 152–154
indirect lighting, 76
ink and paint, 59, 65
interpolation, 63
intracoded frame, 138
inverse discrete cosine transform
      (IDCT), 127
issuer, 53
iterative hashing, 32–33

J

jaggies, 66, 80, 89, 109, 112
Joint Photography Experts Group, 123
JPEG, 123–136
    adjusting quality, 135
    compressing pixel blocks, 132
    compression ratio, 135
    DCT, 125
    picture quality, 135–136
Jurassic Park, 57–58

K

Kerckhoffs's principle, 4, 5, 27, 33
key (encryption), 4
    AES, 9–14
    asymmetric, 38
    code book, 9
    expansion, 9
    keyed hashing, 55
    MAC, 55
    private, 38, 44, 45, 50
    public, 38, 43, 44, 45, 50
    related-key attack, 17
    shared key problem, 18, 37
    size, 20, 47
    symmetric, 18
key (search), 146, 151
key expansion, 9
keyframe, 59
known-plaintext attack, 6

L

Lady and the Tramp, 59
LaserDisc, 116
LCD (liquid crystal display), 60
light-emitting diode (LED), 60
lighting, 71–80
    ambient, 96–97
    angle of incidence, 74, 75
    angle of reflectance, 74
    bump mapping, 106, 107

diffuse reflection, 74, 77, 92, 93, 107
direct, 76
distance effect, 72–73, 92
indirect, 76
model, 72
normal, 92, 93, 107
ray tracing. *See* ray tracing
real-time, 92–97
reflection, 80
    clear, 103
    environment mapping, 103–105
shadow. *See* shadow
specular reflection, 75, 77, 92, 107
link farming, 159
links
    farming, 159
    inbound, 158
    pass-through, 159
liquid-crystal display (LCD), 60
local coordinate, 62
lossless compression, 116
lossy compression, 116, 124
luminance, 124

M

MAC, 55
macroblock, 139
    deblocking filter, 143
man-in-the-middle attack, 52, 56
map
    converting to table, 176
    directed graph, 176
    routing. *See* routing
massively multiplayer online
        game (MMO), 164
master secret, 54
matrix, 128
matrix multiplication, 126
MD5, 21–25
    digital signature, 25–26
    encoding password for, 21–22
    quality of, 25
    round, 24–25
message authentication code, 55
mipmap, 102
MMO (massively multiplayer
        online game), 164
model, 61–63, 70, 87
    ambient light, 96
    bump mapping, 106
    control point, 62
    distant impostor, 106
    drawing, transforming into, 62, 88,
        93, 105

global illumination, 76
    interpolation, 63
    lighting, 72
    line, 62
    scaling, 64
    tessellation, 107–108
    translation, 64
Mortal Kombat, 85
movie-quality rendering, 70, 82–83
MPEG-2, 138–142
    adjusting quality, 139
    B-frame, 139
    GOP, 138, 142
    I-frame, 138, 139
    macroblock, 139
    P-frame, 139
MPEG-4, 143
multisample anti-aliasing (MSAA),
        110–111
    vs. supersampling, 111
multitasking, 162–163, 174

N

nearest-neighbor sampling, 99–100,
        101, 143
normal, 92, 93, 107
NOT (bitwise operation), 23, 25
numerical address, 153

O

offset, 139
one-time pad, 9
one-way function, 39, 42
optical printer, 82
OR (bitwise operation), 23, 25
origin, 61

P

packet, 118
painter's algorithm, 90
partition, 147
pass-through link, 159
password, 6, 19
    common, 28, 29
    encoding, 21–22
    hashing, 20–23
    salt, 34, 35
    storage service, 35–36
    table, 26, 27
performance scaling, 150
persistence of vision, 59
P-frame, 139

T

tabula recta, 7
temporal compression, 138
temporal redundancy, 138, 142
tessellation, 107–108
test-and-set, 169
texel, 98
texture mapping, 97–103, 143
    bump mapping, 106
    sampling, 97
TGA file format, 117
    compression ratio, 118
    packet, 118
Theora, 143
timing attack, 17
tombstone, 156
Toon Boom, 69
Toonz, 69
totient, 43, 45
transaction, 164, 166–167
translation, 64
translucency, 68, 78
transposition, 2–6
    rotation, 14
trapdoor function, 40
triangle, 88, 90, 107
trilinear filtering, 102–103, 143
trivial factor, 40
tweening, 59
    automatic, 63–64

U

ultra high definition video (UHD), 144

V

variable-size storage, 152, 153
vector, 126
video streaming, 116
videocassette, 115
view angle, 74
viewpoint, 71
virtual camera, 71

W

War and Peace, 122
web search, 157–160
web session, 52
world coordinate, 70, 88
write semaphore, 173

X

x-axis, 61
x-coordinate, 61
XOR (bitwise operation), 11, 14, 15

Y

y-axis, 61
YCbCr color system, 124
    vs. RGB, 124
y-coordinate, 61
Y (luminance), 124

Z

z-coordinate, 69
.zip file format, 122